The Prairie Table Cookbook

Bill Kurtis with Michelle M. Martin

SOURCEBOOKS, INC.®
NAPERVILLE, ILLINOIS

Published by Sourcebooks, Inc.
P.O. Box 4410, Naperville, Illinois 60567-4410
(630) 961-3900
Fax: (630) 961-2168
www.sourcebooks.com

Library of Congress Cataloging-in-Publication Data

Kurtis, Bill.
  The prairie table cookbook / Bill Kurtis.
    p. cm.
  Includes bibliographical references.
  1. Cookery, American--Western style. 2. Cookery (Beef) 3. Cookery (Buffalo meat) 4. Cookery (Natural foods) 5. Natural beef. I. Tallgrass Beef Co. II. Title.

TX715.2.W47K87 2007
641.5978--dc22

                          2007027397

              Printed and bound in United States of America.
                  BG 10 9 8 7 6 5 4 3 2 1

contents

Acknowledgments:

The Round Up vii

Introduction:

The Tallgrass Beef Odyssey: Bill Kurtis 1

Prairie Cooking Today: Michelle Martin 7

Chapter 1:

The American Indian Prairie Table 11

   Native American Recipes 15

      Fried Meat Pies 19

      Chi-bonne' Hamburger 19

      Pemmican 20

   The Tallgrass Cattle Drive 22

Chapter 2:

Dining with the Army 25

   Military Recipes 29

      Irish Stew 35

      Buffalo Tongue 35

      Fort Laramie Slumgullion 36

      Texacus 37

      Spanish Steak 37

      Hardtack (Hardcrackers) 38

      Army Bread Recipe 39

      Dried Bean Soup (from Stock) 40

      Bombshells 41

      Fricassee of Beef 42

Why the Prairie. 43

Chapter 3:

Moving West 47

Prairie Settlers' Recipes 49

Meat Loaf. 56

Meat Rocks. 56

Flank Steak 57

Mrs. Peaks's Pineapple Cucumber Salad 57

Beef à-la-Mode 58

Helen's Baked Hash 60

Lucine's Five-Hour Stew 60

Lynch's Famous Chili 61

Liver and Onions 62

Apple Dumplings 63

Good Brown Stew (Cooked in the Iron Dutch Oven) 64

Chili Stew 65

Fresh Mountain Oysters 65

Barbecue Style Meatloaf 66

Beef Jerky 66

The Magic of Grass 68

Chapter 4:

The Cowboy Table on the Trail 71

Ranch and Trail Recipes 76

Ranch House Pot Roast 83

Chuck Wagon Bean Soup with Beef 83

Frying Pan Supper. 84

Pan Fried Steaks 85

Helava Chili 86

Chuck Wagon Scrapple 87

Splatterdabs 88
Corn Fritters 88
Rice and Onions 89
Cowboy Beans 89
Chuck Wagon Stew 90
Bacon and Beans 91
Chili Beef 92
Sourdough Starter 92
Sourdough Biscuits 93
Confederate Coffee Cake 94
Beef Tips 95
Smothered Steak 95
Beef Tenders 96
Texas Beef Tips 96
Roast Beef 97
Cowpoke Beans 97
Ketcham Canyon Stew 98
Sage Biscuits 99
Why I'm a Grass-Fed Beef Rancher 100

Chapter 5:
The Modern Prairie Table 107
Recipes from Famous Cowboys and Great Chefs 107
Broccoli-Cauliflower Salad 108
Beef Roll-Ups with Whiskey Butter Sauce 109
Cowboy Steaks in a Skillet 110
Will Rogers's Favorite Chili 112
Gene Autry's Homemade Meatloaf 113
Dale Evans's Quick Chili-Tex 113
Frank Phillips's Pheasant à la King (Revised 3/11/1948) 114
Baxter Black's Beans à la Black (A recipe for trouble) 117

Governor Kathleen Sebelius's Filet of Beef Bourguignon 119

Mayor Jim Sherer's Mom's Recipe for Chicken Fried Steak 121

Filet Mignon with Cabernet Peppercorn Sauce 123

Grilled Ribeye Steaks 124

Grilled Lime Marinated Flank Steak with Chipotle Honey Sauce 125

Strip Steak with Rosemary Red Wine Sauce 126

Sarah Stegner and George Bumbaris's Tallgrass New York Strip Steak
     with Shallot Herb Topping 127

Sarah Stegner and George Bumbaris's Shepherd's Pie Prairie Grass Café Style 128

Paul Katz's 8-oz Tallgrass Filet with Lobster Mashed Potatoes
     and Red Wine Demi Glace 129

Paul Katz's Homemade Veal Stock 131

Rick Bayless's Bistec Encebollado (Slivered Beef with Well-Browned Onions) 132

Michel Nischan's Beef Short Rib Pot Roast 134

David Burns's Braised Tallgrass Beef Short Ribs (Asian-Style with
     Baby Bok Choy, Shiitake Mushrooms, and Jasmine Rice) 136

Colin Crowley's Black Pepper–Crusted Standing Rib Roast au Jus 138

Colin Crowley's Whole Roasted Beef Sirloin with Chasseur Sauce 140

Colin Crowley's Beef Bourguignon 141

Colin Crowley's Braised Short Ribs with Morel Mushroom
     and Cannellini Bean Ragout 142

Charlie Trotter's Grilled Beef Tenderloin Cobb Salad 144

A Day in the Saddle on the Red Buffalo Ranch 146

Resources

Experience the West 149

Chapter Notes 150

Photo Credits 152

Photo Descriptions 152

The Round Up

This book was born in January 2006 around a conference table at the headquarters for Tallgrass Beef Company in Sedan, Kansas. At the time, it seemed like an easy task to publish a cookbook that brought together good recipes that could be made even better by using Tallgrass Beef. The more we thought about Tallgrass Beef and our vision for a healthier food product for the American consumer we were struck with one amazing fact—Americans in earlier generations had eaten this healthy, wholesome beef long before we rediscovered it! Going back to the past for inspiration connects us to the present and the mission of Tallgrass Beef Company. Through good sleuthing work and the help of many individuals, this book is the realization of a dream. Several state, county, and local historical societies and organizations were instrumental in providing information and assistance as we compiled our materials. Thanks to the following organizations and historical sites in Kansas for their gracious help with materials and assistance: Baxter Springs Heritage Center and Museum, Center for Great Plains Studies at Emporia State University, Chase County Historical Society, Dodge City Convention and Visitors Bureau, Drover's Mercantile in Ellsworth, Flying W Ranch, Fort Scott National Historic Site, Kansas State Historical Society, Kansas Cattle Town Coalition, Little House on the Prairie, and Tallgrass Prairie Preserve; in Missouri: the Roy Rogers and Dale Evans Museum; in Oklahoma: the Ball Ranch, the Chisholm Trail Heritage Center in Duncan, National Cowboy and Western Heritage Museum in Oklahoma City, Oklahoma Historical Society in Oklahoma City, Prairie Song in Dewey, Will Rogers Memorial and Museum in Claremore, the Woolaroc Ranch, Museum, and Wildlife Preserve in Bartlesville; in Texas: the Palo Duro Canyon State Park and the Panhandle Plains Historical Museum in Canyon; and in California: the Autry Center for the Study of the American West and Autry Entertainment.

Numerous individuals were also instrumental in helping bring this book to life through their assistance and support. Marva Felchlin at the Autry Center; Maxine Hansen and Jackie Autry at Autry Entertainment; Larry O'Neill at the Baxter Springs Heritage Center; Jim Hoy at the Center for Great Plains Studies; John Hoy at the Flying W Ranch in Cedar Point, Kansas; Mayor Jim Sherer of Dodge City, Kansas; Kansas Governor Kathleen Sebelius; Rosemary Frey and Alan Chilton at Fort Scott National Historic Site; Arnold Schofield at Mine Creek Battlefield; Dennis Katzenmeier and the Kansas Cattle Town Coalition; Nancy Sherbut (photographs), Lin Fredericksen (manuscripts), and the research room staff at the Kansas State Historical Society; Joanna Stratton; Dick and Nita

Jones, and Judy Tolbert of Sedan, Kansas; Chris and Cathi Ball at the Ball Ranch near Bowring, Oklahoma; Cova Williams at the Chisholm Trail Heritage Center; Connie Pruitt, David Keathly, and Jack Keathly of Ponca City, Oklahoma; Chuck Rand at the National Cowboy and Western Heritage Museum; Terry Zinn at the Oklahoma Historical Society; Kenneth and Marilyn Moore Tate at Prairie Song; Steven Graggert at Will Rogers Memorial Museum; Bob Fraser, Ken Meek, and Linda Stone at Woolaroc Ranch, Museum, and Wildlife Preserve; Trammel and Susan Rushing and the Rushing Wagon of El Reno, Oklahoma; Matt Cravey of Canyon, Texas, for an excellent afternoon in the Palo Duro Canyon; and Betty Bustos at Panhandle Plains Historical Museum.

The true heroes of this book, however, are the men and women that blazed the trails into the West. Those brave souls endured hardship and despair to create a world anew in the West that offered them a life of freedom. We hope you will enjoy this journey into the West as we sit down at the prairie table together.

The Tallgrass Beef Odyssey

Several centuries back, when the spring wind blew from the southwest across the vast American prairie, Indian tribes would set fire to the land. They burned away dead vegetation to speed the way for green shoots to emerge and attract buffalo. Sometimes the fire would get out of control, belching flames against the black night sky and devouring anything in its path. The Osage Indians called it the "red buffalo."

There's a new prairie fire sweeping across America. This red buffalo also has the power to change the landscape because it blows up from the people. The belching flames are voices raising concern that something is wrong with the way we eat. The green shoots of grass are expressions of hope that there is a more natural way to eat, one that can bring pleasure as well as health and harmony with the land. This book is part of that movement and shows how some are moving ahead by traveling backward.

I founded Tallgrass Beef Company when the words organic, natural, pasture-raised, and free-range confused more than they defined. Cattle could be organic and still be confined in feedlots and fed only corn for six months of their lives—if the corn was organic. Natural was presumed to mean animals raised without antibiotics or growth hormones, but the animal could still be confined to a feedlot and fed corn. Pasture-raised presumably meant that cattle never left the pasture but it really meant a rancher could qualify if he left the corral gate open. Free-range came closer to the concept, except that animals could be fed corn in a pasture instead of a feedlot.

I came upon another term that I thought more accurately expressed what I was looking for—grass-fed and grass-finished beef. It's pretty hard to interpret that as anything but pure. It means beef cattle are raised only in pasture, receive no growth hormones, no antibiotics, and no grain as feed. They eat only grass and natural supplements, such as minerals.

As a conservationist, I wanted to bring sustainability to my ranch in Kansas and raising grass-fed and grass-finished beef seemed to be the perfect fit. It was good for the land (the cattle fertilize the next year's native grasses), good for the animals that live the life for which they were designed (grazing pastures), and good for family farmers who had been forced into a grain-based commodity system that had few alternatives—and good for us, for whom grass-fed beef presents a remarkable package of health benefits and the original taste of beef.

But the challenge was daunting. There was no market for grass-fed beef. Although many had tried,

few had been able to succeed beyond selling to friends. They could raise cattle on grass—ranchers know cattle—but they couldn't sell them as easily. Markets are built one restaurant and one butcher at a time. And corn-fed cattle had taken over the market. Times had changed.

Although there were some feedlots around in 1885, the modern corn-fed revolution gained momentum during World War II. The U.S. government gave surplus corn to ranchers who fed it to their cattle and found that the extra intra-muscular fat that produced marbling in the muscles made the meat taste good. In addition, the corn's starch enabled them to gain weight faster. To the beef industry, those corn kernels amounted to gold nuggets.

Over the next sixty years, the entire beef industry in America changed over to a corn-fed diet. Since we in the U.S. believe that bigger is better, the cattlemen created giant feedlots to fatten the cattle after they had been weaned at six to ten months of age. In the Texas panhandle, a group of four confined animal feeding operations (CAFOs) can fatten 250,000 cattle at once. Always looking for ways to increase production, growth hormones were added to make the cattle gain even more weight—faster. But the abrupt change in diet from grass to corn created problems. First, there is bloating. Corn ferments in a cow's digestive tract. Fermentation in the animal's rumen produces gas. If the cow can't belch it away fast enough, it can suffocate. Then comes acidosis, which can lead to diarrhea, ulcers, liver disease, and a variety of feedlot diseases that come with confining cattle for five to six months. Still, the feedlot operators found an answer—antibiotics keep the animals alive for the confined months until they can be harvested. To enable its massive growth over the last sixty years, the livestock industry has reached a point where it uses more than 75 percent of all the antibiotics manufactured in the United States.

Life seemed good for the beef industry. Fast food drove the demand for more and more beef. Steak houses seemed to appear on every corner. Beef was the number one source of protein, and America's favorite meal.

But the good news wouldn't last. What seemed like a win-win advance sixty years ago was vulnerable to new forces in the marketplace. Feedlots that kept animals jammed into small paddocks were attacked for a lack of animal compassion. Despite the industry's continued protests, the growth hormones were widely believed to cause obesity in general, and early puberty in young girls. The European Union banned American beef from cattle that had been given hormones. A number of scientists claimed that "superbugs" resistant to antibiotics used in livestock had been found in humans. Cases of *E. coli* poisoning were traced to beef and drew new scrutiny of the industry.

The industry was listening. Millions of dollars in research was devoted to improving the feedlot system. And the demand for all things natural fueled a new movement, one that respected the integrity of the animals and the land. Some ranchers embraced the quick and easy steps of eliminating growth hormones and the use of antibiotics for anything other than treating illness. They expressed a desire to be more compassionate to their animals by giving them more pasture time and using facilities designed to reduce stress. But a rancher can do those things and still finish cattle on corn, believing America has developed a taste for a corn-fed, highly marbled steak (without considering that's the only choice we've had). It hardly seems natural to continue an unnatural diet of corn, but that compromise was a stepping stone to the real prize—a return to the diet for which cows were designed—grass.

My epiphany came when I began to read the scientific data. Fossil records trace the bovine species back several million years, but for the purpose of this book let's start about thirty thousand years ago in France's Chauvet Cave. There on the walls in breathtaking detail are cattle, complete with horns and body shape similar to the breeds of today. Someone thought enough of what paleo-anthropologists know as *aurochs* (an early bovine species) to paint them above all other choices. They appear again twelve thousand years ago in Lascaux Cave.

Professor Loren Cordain of Colorado State University, and author of *The Paleo Diet*, writes, "[B]y analyzing stable isotopes of various elements in fossilized *hominin* bones and contrasting these signatures to isotopes in known prey animals, it is possible to determine the relative proportion of prey animals in the diet of the predator." He found that the flesh of *Bovinae* (including *aurochs*) comprised 58 percent of the meat consumed by early man, including Neanderthals. If early man (hominin) ate the cattle, what did the cattle eat? Grass—until corn replaced their diet sixty years ago. We evolved on a diet of grass-fed animals.

The relatively new academic discipline of evolutionary medicine argues, according to Dr. Cordain, that "the profound changes in the environment that began . . . approximately ten thousand years ago occurred too recently on an evolutionary timescale for the human genome to adjust." So, our bodies

expect the nutrition of the grass-fed diet. But they are getting a corn-fed diet. What's the problem?

Corn feeding may be adversely affecting our health. Corn-fed animals have high total fat, and that's the saturated kind of fat we're told is bad for us. Corn-fed beef has a low omega-3 fatty acid content with high omega-6 fatty acids. The result is a fatty acid ratio that is out of balance with what the evolutionary grass-fed diet dictates. "Many of the current health problems and chronic diseases which afflict the American public result from excessive consumption of refined sugars, grains, vegetable oils, fatty meats, and dairy products," according to Dr. Cordain. "Human health and well being could potentially be improved by including more lean grass-fed beef in the U.S. diet . . . ." The Union of Concerned Scientists notes in the report *Greener Pastures*, issued in March 2006, "Grain-based diets can also promote virulent strains of *E. coli* in the digestive tract. Cattle switched from corn to hay for even brief periods before slaughter are less likely to contaminate beef products with harmful *E. coli* during processing" (Russell and Rychlik, 2001). A modern grass-fed cow is much like a grass-fed animal that grazed thousands of years ago. Because its meat is lower in fat than the grain-fed animals, it is also lower in calories. *The Journal of Animal Science* reported that a six-ounce steak from a grass-finished steer can have one hundred fewer calories than a six-ounce steak from a grain-fed steer. If you're a typical beef eater consuming 66.5 pounds a year, "switching to lean grass-fed beef will save you 17,733 calories a year" (*The Journal of Animal Science* 80.5:1202–11).

How about those omega-3s? Jo Robinson, a noted proponent of grass-fed beef, writes that meat from grass-fed animals has two to four times more omega-3 fatty acids than grain-fed meat. Omega-3s have become the darling of nutritionists. Discovered in 1972, they are considered essential to good health but they have been squeezed out of our western diet because they are associated with fresh foods. Our modern, overly refined, over-processed diet is designed to extend shelf life instead of freshness, and titillate our taste buds with salts and sugars to sell more products instead of delivering the original, genuine taste of real food. The benefits of a diet with high amounts of omega-3s include: reduced chance of developing high blood pressure; a 50 percent decrease in the odds of suffering a heart attack; a decrease in the odds of suffering from depression, schizophrenia, attention deficit disorder (ADD), or Alzheimer's disease. It helps the immune system and helps prevent arthritis. It may even reduce the risk of cancer.

Imagine your doctor saying, "Eat more beef." The common recommended sources for omega-3 are cold water fish like salmon, nuts like walnuts and almonds, and flax seeds ground up as a fiber supplement. What has not reached the attention of many nutritionists is that grass-fed, pasture-raised livestock are also a wonderful source, especially when one tires of fish. "Omega-3s are formed in the chloroplasts of green leaves and algae. Sixty percent of the fatty acids in grass are omega-3s," Jo Robinson said at Eatwild.com. "Each day that an animal spends in the feedlot, its supply of omega-3s is diminished." Fresh pasture-raised animals also have three to five times the amount of conjugated linoleic acid or CLA, a fatty acid discovered in 1987. Unfortunately it has been eliminated in our low-fat diets. It is apparently produced by bacteria in the rumen of grass-eating animals. Believers follow the advice of Dr. Tilak Dhiman of Utah State University, who advocates drinking one glass of whole milk, eating one ounce of cheese and one serving of grass-fed beef to lower your risk of cancer.

You can see why my head was turned toward raising cattle on grass even though nearly thirty million head of cattle in America's herd annually will end up in the grain/corn concentrated feed operations. But there is one more test—taste. Taste is in the buds of the individual, of course. Some beef eaters have never known the original taste of beef from a grass-fed animal. They were reared on that juicy, corn-fed, highly marbled piece of meat and all the health benefits in the world won't make a difference if the taste is "a little funny." But the fact is that superb taste can be found in the original English breeds that started out on grass because they have

the right genetics. It's the way they were supposed to be all along. Leaner yes, but the taste is in the meat, not the fat.

It's one part of the natural/organic movement, now sweeping over us like a red buffalo prairie fire, growing at the rate of 20 percent a year. Very soon, it will reach a tipping point when America's entire agri-business industry will be forced to reconsider the quality of the food it produces. Because the people demand it.

We haven't chosen the easiest trail. But we've pointed our herd north toward Kansas in an effort to find a new market for an old product. We call it Tallgrass Beef, a grass-fed and grass-finished product.

And these are a few of our stories along the trail.

Bill Kurtis

Prairie Cooking Today

What we eat is just as much a part of our history as the events and personalities that shaped the West. While researching this work we discovered that beef has always been an American tradition. The recipes and cooking methods may have changed, but the desire for fresh, tender, succulent beef has not.

Many of the recipes here are reproduced exactly as originally worded, even if they appear incorrect by today's standards of grammar. And we have taken great care to preserve the integrity of the recipes as much as possible. In the nineteenth century, people cooked primarily outdoors in Dutch ovens over open fires. When cooking stoves became more prevalent, cooking was transferred inside on metal cook tops and eventually on baking racks in wood and gas burning stoves.

The historical chapters will give you a glimpse of American life in the West during the great cattle trade era, as well as a better appreciation of our modern conveniences. While many of the historical recipes can be adapted and prepared in the modern kitchen, some are presented purely as historical artifacts, much like the historical photographs that appear throughout the book. These appear in a green box, with ingredients and method in paragraphs, as opposed to "adaptable" recipes which are presented with a list of ingredients separate from method.

If items were cooked in Dutch ovens over any level of heat, use your stove top and a Dutch oven or modern cookware. If items were baked in a Dutch oven you can, of course, bake them in your modern stove and use a heat appropriate for the item being baked. If you are adventurous, try cooking some of these items on a camping trip over the open fire, especially some of the recipes in chapter four, "The

Cowboy Table." There is nothing better than the smell of the crackling fire and cowboy chuck to make you appreciate the cowboy way of life.

In the nineteenth century, lard was one of the primary ingredients used to cook, and was also rendered down to make candles and lye soap. Instead of using lard to prepare the historical recipes, use your favorite heart healthy oils instead.

Spices were ever present in the recipes of the nineteenth century. What pioneer and chuck wagon cooks lacked in supply or variety, they more than made up for in taste. The spices used in the nineteenth-century recipes are still available today at your supermarket. Try using fresh garlic, cloves, thyme, marjoram, and dried and rubbed sage—the flavors of the West will come alive on the tip of your tongue.

Most of these recipes use beef as their main ingredient. You can substitute Tallgrass Beef wherever you see beef or bison as ingredients. Grass-fed, grass-finished beef is not only naturally healthy but also the true beef of the American West. While traveling from Texas to market in Kansas, cattle grazed on grasses, particularly in the bluestem region of Kansas, a rich land for finishing cattle. Each bite of Tallgrass Beef takes you back to an earlier, simpler time in our history when food was free of chemicals and preservatives.

chapter 1

The American Indian Prairie Table

I walked out three miles, found the prarie composed of good Land and plenty of water roleing and interspursed with points of timbered land, Those Praries are not open like those, or a number of those E. of the Mississippi Void of every thing except grass, they abound with Hasel Grapes and a wild plumb of a Superior size and quallity, called the Osages Plumb. Grows on a bush the hight of a Hasel and is three times the sise of other Plumbs, and hang in great quantities on the bushes I Saw great numbers of Deer in the Praries, the evening is Cloudy, our party in high Spirits.

—JOURNAL OF WILLIAM CLARK, JUNE 10, 1804

With the stroke of a pen, President Thomas Jefferson doubled the size of the young American nation when he purchased the wild, untapped Louisiana Territory from Napoleon Bonaparte of France. He couldn't explore it himself so he dispatched Captain William Clark and Lieutenant Meriwether Lewis to be his eyes and ears. Carrying peace medals, blankets, beads, and assorted

visages are broad, which tend to strengthen the idea of their being giants.

French and Spanish trappers, traders, explorers, and missionaries had long understood the nutritive value of American Indian foodstuffs as they traversed the West. As Lewis and Clark's Corps of Discovery entered this wonderland, they too sampled the local foods: beans, pumpkins, squash, wild potatoes, and, from the Pawnee, corn. Corn was central to the Pawnee religious beliefs. Their most sacred bundles contained two ears of corn representative of their "great mother." The most important Pawnee ceremonies were held to ensure a bountiful corn crop. With the discovery of silver on the American River in California in 1848 and gold in the Black Hills of South Dakota in the 1860s, settlers took full advantage of the variety within the American Indian diet.

I had been over the line before, when I saw the immense herds of buffalo migrating south. I had read descriptions of those annual migrations and can only repeat the usual statement that there seemed to be millions of the mighty brutes. For some twelve or fifteen miles to the northward, the prairie seemed literally covered with them as far as the eye could see.

—ADOLPH ROENIGK, KANSAS SETTLER, 1868

trinkets they kept detailed journals of their daily progress and observations of the vast lands that would become the American West. Their maps, sketches, and descriptions of the land and its inhabitants would be the first accounts that Americans living east of the Mississippi would behold. And what an astonishing view it was: treeless, grassy prairies seemed to roll endlessly to the very end of the sky itself; millions upon millions of bison used the entire mid-continent as their pastures; and nomadic tribes partnered with horses to live off the ancient beasts. Among the most striking of these people were the Osage, located in present day Kansas and Oklahoma. Even before Lewis and Clark, explorers like John Bradbury, an Englishman, described them in mythical terms:

The Osages are so tall and robust as almost to warrant the application of the term gigantic: few of them appear to be under six feet, and many are above it. Their shoulders and

Adolph Roenigk wrote these words in 1868 during a time of immense change in Kansas. The American Civil War was over. Former soldiers, both Union and Confederate, were migrating to the fertile plains of Kansas to seek healing from the battle scars inflicted east of the Mississippi. Kansas earned the moniker "The Soldier State" as waves of these blue-and-grey-clad warriors turned muskets into ploughshares that broke the virgin soil. The European way of life slowly replaced the rich horse culture of the Plains Indians. One consequence was that the spectacular herds of buffalo that Roenigk described were decimated by white hunters and with them, the Native American way of life. The buffalo meant everything to the tribes of the plains—everything that was needed to live and survive the harsh extremes of life on the prairie. Songs, poems, stories, and artwork reflect the central role of the buffalo in American Indian life. The Sun Dance, for example, utilized the skull of a buffalo on the top of a large pole as a focal point for sun dancers to gather around while performing the dance.

Some tribes, the Osage included, were resilient. They filled the empty buffalo pastures with new grazing animals—cattle. In Indian Territory along the border between Kansas and present day Oklahoma, the Osages keenly understood that the lush, green, nutritious grasses of the Flint Hills could fatten cattle driven from Texas to Kansas for shipping to hungry consumers in the East. While Indian agents further west were struggling to convert other tribes to the agricultural way of life, the Osage embraced ranching which was, in many respects, closer to the lifestyle they had known following migratory herds of buffalo.

THE INDIAN AND THE BUFFALO

THE BUFFALO WAS THE DEPARTMENT STORE OF THE PLAINS INDIAN. THE FLESH WAS FOOD, THE BLOOD WAS DRINK, SKINS FURNISHED WIGWAMS, ROBES MADE BLANKETS AND BEDS, DRESSED HIDES SUPPLIED MOCCASINS AND CLOTHING, HAIR WAS TWISTED INTO ROPES, RAWHIDE BOUND TOOLS TO HANDLES, GREEN HIDES MADE POTS FOR COOKING OVER BUFFALO-CHIP FIRES, HIDES FROM BULLS' NECKS MADE SHIELDS THAT WOULD TURN ARROWS, RIBS WERE RUNNERS FOR DOG-DRAWN SLEDS, SMALL BONES WERE AWLS AND NEEDLES, FROM HOOVES CAME GLUE FOR FEATHERING ARROWS, FROM SINEWS CAME THREAD AND BOWSTRINGS, FROM HORNS CAME BOWS, CUPS AND SPOONS, AND EVEN FROM GALLSTONES A "MEDICINE" PAINT WAS MADE. WHEN THE MILLIONS OF BUFFALO THAT ROAMED THE PRAIRIES WERE EXTERMINATED, THE PLAINS TRIBES WERE STARVED INTO SUBMISSION.

—KANSAS HISTORICAL MARKER
AT HIGHWAY 50 SOUTH NEAR GARDEN CITY,
KANSAS, IN FINNEY COUNTY

Native American Recipes

American Indian cooking included many items that the average prairie traveler found strange. Chokecherries, mulberries, persimmons, pawpaws, wild plumbs, and prairie turnips were an important part of the American Indian diet. Buffalo, deer, turkey, elk, and other game provided protein in the diet. The act of gathering this bounty also gave young boys the life experiences that transformed them into young men and warriors.

Many of the historical recipes in this chapter are still prepared today by American Indian tribes in Southeast Kansas, Southwest Missouri, and Northwest Oklahoma. In days gone by these recipes would have been prepared in wooden bowls, cast iron skillets, and Dutch ovens. Baking would have been carried out in baking pits, dug into the earth to hold the heat of the fire and glowing coals. Earthen pits were the crock pots of the time period and could be built wherever a tribe was migrating regardless of the time of year.

Some of the following historical recipes are presented as historical artifacts. Some may be adapted for modern kitchens, though the authors do not recommend trapping raccoons!

WE-GI (EGG SOUP)

Beat eggs—chicken or bird—slightly and pour into boiling water. Season with salt and grease meat, if you have it. Serve hot with mush.

—from Ruby East, a Cherokee woman

❧

WILD GRAPE DUMPLINGS

Use Possum Grapes when ripe in the fall. They grow in the woods and along creek banks. Cook one half-gallon wild possum grapes till they are boiling, using just enough water to cover. Strain through a clean sack. Make dumplings out of one half-cup grape juice, two cups flour, two teaspoons baking powder and one teaspoon lard (shortening), by stirring the ingredients to make stiff dough. Add a tablespoon or two more of grape juice, if needed. Sweeten the boiling grape juice left and boil in juice.

—from Ruby East, a Cherokee woman

❧

AH HAH JUMBA TUKLAYGEE (GRITTED SWEET POTATOES)

In the nineteenth century, this dish would have been baked in a Dutch oven over an open fire or in another container placed in a cooking pit.

Take any amount of sweet potatoes that are gritted (peeled), put in a little sugar and flour and roll into a biscuit from the palm of the hand and bake in an oven. These are called sweet potato biscuits.

—from Ruby East, a Cherokee woman

Pxashikana (Dried Meat)

Cut lean meat (deer, elk, buffalo) into long, flat, narrow strips about two inches wide. Cut with the grain of the meat.

Hang these strips on a green wood pole four to five feet high in the hot sun. Build a smoldering fire underneath (or downwind) using hickory wood, if possible. Keep the flames down by sprinkling with water from time to time. This will season the meat and keep the insects away. Turn the meat strips from time to time. Keep smoking until dry and stiff. Takes about one day or a bit longer, if not really sunny.

Seminole Parched Corn

Have a pit dug (about four feet by ten feet wide). Build a fire and burn this until half full of coals. Take any amount of roasting ears, shucked, and place a long iron on top of the pit and lay corn on it. Watch and turn over until corn is done. Shell or cut from cob and dry out in the hot sun. This next part of the recipe is for winter use: This can be cooked together with singed cleaned squirrels and some port or other meat (beef, buffalo, deer) drippings. The fresh corn can be made by boiling it on the cob or cut and dry as parched corn.

Indian Baked Raccoon

Remove skin and inner parts of raccoon, singe over fire and wash. Then parboil for one hour. Then place in roaster in about three inches of hot water. Add one each—carrot, apple, and onion. Bake until tender.

POKE

Poke, or pokeweed, is a common vegetable weed still eaten in parts of the South today, despite containing toxins which may be harmful to humans. Native Americans used its purple berries for dye to decorate horses. This recipe was also used with dandelions and other native greens and edible grasses and plants.

Wash young tender shoots of poke (stalk and leaves). Place in a saucepan and boil for fifteen to twenty minutes. Drain and fry in grease till tender. Serve hot using vinegar as a sauce.

SCRAPPLE

Scrapple is a delicious breakfast dish. Take the head, heart, and any lean scraps of pork and boil until the flesh slips easily from the bones. Remove the fat, gristle, and bones. Set the liquid in which the meat was boiled aside until cold; take the cake of fat from the surface and return it to the fire. Let it boil again, then thicken with corn meal as you would in making ordinary corn meal mush, by letting it slip through the fingers slowly to prevent lumps. Cook an hour, stirring constantly at first, afterwards putting back on the fire (or range) in a position to boil gently. When thick enough to mould, pour into a long square pan, not too deep. When cold, cut into slices and fry until golden brown, as you do mush. Roll in seasoned flour.

Fried Meat Pies

- 1 ½ pounds of round steak, ground coarse with a little suet, salt, and pepper to taste

Make a batter of:
- 2 cups flour
- 3 teaspoons baking powder
- 1 teaspoon salt
- Enough sweet milk or warm water to make the batter very thick

Make meat balls about the size of a large walnut. Drop in batter and coat well, then place them in a kettle of hot fat as for doughnuts.

Chi-bonne' Hamburger

- ½ pound hamburger
- 2 large onion slices
- Salt and pepper
- 1 pat of butter

Campers might find this recipe a useful way to prepare hamburgers ahead of time for the campfire. The foil-wrapped burger patties can be tossed directly into the fire.

Grease aluminum foil with butter. Make 1 large hamburger or 2 small ones. Place onion slices on hamburger. Salt and pepper and add remaining butter. Wrap hamburger(s) and seal tightly with foil. Place on coals from a fire, onion side up. Turn occasionally. Cook for 15 minutes.

Pemmican

- 2 pounds of lean buffalo, elk, or beef loin
- 1 ½ pounds of dried currant berries
- Molasses to sweeten and for binding

Cut meat into thin slices about ⅟₁₆ to ⅛-inch thick. Hang to dry for 2 to 4 days until thoroughly dry (for safety, follow current jerky or curing methods). Pulverize dried meat to fine, almost powdery flakes. Add dried currant berries and mix well. Add molasses to sweeten and bind mixture. Mix well and knead into a big dough-like ball. Pull chunks of big ball and roll into smaller fifty-cent size balls, then flatten them. Let sit for 2 days to dry. Eat as trail snacks. Will last for years.

In his work *The Prairie Traveler*, Randolph P. Marcy noted that pemmican "can be eaten raw, and many prefer it so. Mixed with a little flour and boiled, it is very wholesome and exceedingly nutritious food, and will keep fresh for a long time." Marcy lauded the value of pemmican and gave his own recipe for the protein-rich energy food of the prairie. By today's standards the use of a "bag of the animal's hide" and melted grease, most likely lard, hardly seems health conscious.

The pemmican, which constitutes almost the entire diet of the Fur Company's men in the Northwest, is prepared as follows: The buffalo meat is cut into thin flakes, and hung up to dry in the sun or before a slow fire; it is then pounded between two stones and reduced to a powder; this powder is placed in a bag of the animal's hide, with the hair on the outside; melted grease is then poured into it, and the bag sewn up.

As the West became populated with settlers, gold seekers, soldiers, land speculators, and immigrants from around the globe, the ecosystem in which the buffalo had thrived was rapidly changing. The coming of the Conestoga, teams of oxen, steel plows, and European communities meant the western prairie would never be the same.

THE RISING OF THE BUFFALO MEN

(FROM THE OSAGE RITE OF VIGIL)

I rise, I rise, I, whose tread makes the
    earth to rumble.

I rise, I rise, I, in whose thighs there
    is strength.

I rise, I rise, I, who whips his back
    with his tail when in rage.

I rise, I rise, I, in whose humped
    shoulder there is power.

I rise, I rise, I, who shakes his mane
    when angered.

I rise, I rise, I, whose horns are sharp
    and curved.

The Tallgrass Cattle Drive

Dreams abound in America. That's what makes us great. In 1867, entrepreneur Joseph McCoy had a bold idea. It came to him when he was a livestock trader in Chicago witnessing the new technology of the day—railroads—transform the American West. If he could attract the great cattle herds moving out of Texas to an intersection with the railroads through Kansas, he could multiply his business tenfold, maybe a hundredfold.

The intersecting point on the plains of Kansas was in Abilene, in the grass-rich Flint Hills. McCoy spent $5,000 on advertising and riders to carry promotional posters to the Texas herds of longhorns already heading north. He promised that he would pay more per head in Abilene. He was so true to his word that eventually the whole nation would adopt the phrase, "That's the real McCoy!" One cattleman brought six hundred cows for which he had paid $5,400 and sold them to McCoy for $16,800. And so the cattle drives swung toward Abilene, Kansas. Between 1867 and 1881, McCoy shipped more than two million cattle from Abilene to Chicago, creating the largest stockyards in the world and a city to go with them.

It took an entrepreneur with vision, who was willing to take the risk of applying new technology to an old trade. And it worked. Joseph McCoy gave the young nation an adrenaline rush for its growth across the continent, and in doing so earned a place in history.

We at Tallgrass Beef Company feel a strange kinship with Joseph McCoy, as if we're on a cattle drive heading for Abilene, Kansas.

We're developing a market for McCoy's cattle, the original English breeds that eat grass, not grain. His

use of the latest technology—the railroads—is the equivalent of our website, which enables millions of customers to buy our beef directly.

The most unusual connection is our rediscovery of the power of beef. Just as McCoy's cattle provided the protein that fed a nation, Tallgrass Beef stands ready to realign the diets of millions of Americans, and to provide the taste as well as the health benefits that have been processed out of our food over the last sixty years.

By leaving the cattle in the pasture from birth to harvest, we return to a kind of beef that, whether McCoy realized it or not, amounts to a health food, in addition to fitting the evolution of the cow. Over thousands of years, ruminants, from elephants to bison, developed four-chambered stomachs to break down the hard-stemmed grasses that thrived on full sun and extreme weather conditions all over the world. *Homo sapiens* evolved with those animals and used them for much of our diet. Yes, grass-fed wild animals. Corn was not part of that evolution.

That's why Tallgrass Beef Company is all grass, start to finish, just like Joseph McCoy. We have to create a new market for our product by educating the consumer. At the same time, we have to build a supply among ranchers who share our vision. You see why we feel like we're on a trail drive heading for Joseph McCoy's railhead in Abilene. We do have one advantage. The winds of change are blowing across the prairie. It's a revolution—*the Real McCoy!*

chapter 2

Dining with the Army

Our march today was not as hot and dusty as yesterday, we are now journeying over 'Bleeding Kansas.' Not many farms on our route today; our march was over extensive prairies . . . We marched 20 miles over a large prairie destitute of water, both horses and men suffered for want of it . . . Our ration wagon could not reach us last eve. So the cavalry boys provided themselves with meal and a few tin kettles, so our breakfast consists of boiled meal, we eat it out of corn shucks.

—JOURNAL OF CAPTAIN CHARLES PORTER, KANSAS, 1862

The journal entry of a soldier on the march tells of privation and hardship. Stationed in Kansas during the American Civil War, the experiences of Captain Charles Porter prove the adage of Napoleon Bonaparte: "An army marches on its stomach." The United States Army in the nineteenth century was influenced by Bonaparte more than any other military commander. It embraced the tactics, style of dress, mannerisms, and customs of Napoleon's Grand Army, including his attention to the dietary needs of his soldiers. While army fare was not always filled with variety and of the highest culinary caliber, food was prepared in mass quantities to feed men while in garrison, and at the same time, to be highly portable on the trail.

The United States military maintained a constant presence in the American West. After the passage of the Indian Removal Act of 1830, a frontier line of forts that ran from Fort Snelling, Minnesota, to Fort Jessup, Louisiana, divided the Indian Territory of the West from the United States. By 1835 more than thirty thousand members of the Creek, Choctaw, Cherokee, Shawnee, and Chickasaw nations were living west of the Mississippi. The army's main objective was to keep American settlers on their side of the Permanent Indian Frontier line and keep the peace among those tribes in Indian Territory. With Forts Leavenworth, Scott, Harker, Wallace, Riley, and Zarah in Kansas and Fort Gibson in Oklahoma, the army would quickly become one of the main consumers of fresh, dried, and salted beef in the West. Army Quartermaster contracts attracted some of the nation's first cattle drives from the Southwest. Fresh "beeves on the hoof" made the harrowing six hundred mile trip into Indian Territory (Oklahoma and Kansas) to make many a soldier smile in anticipation of adding a little variety to a lackluster diet.

While in garrison at Fort Scott in 1845, Lieutenant Ewell wrote to his sister Becca about the state of affairs on post, and the fare that he and other officers sampled while living in the relative comfort of Officer's Row: " . . . Two raw tomatoes cut up with one onion in one of the three bit saucers neatly covered by another, some salt in a cup, six cold sweet potatoes and two little pieces of beef dried on the gridiron . . . Yesterday I had a pitcher of buttermilk and grouse both sent to me be by Capt. and Mrs. Swords; the Captain was in as they were sitting the table but declined partaking. If it were not for the

kindness of some of the ladies I should fare badly." While Ewell may have felt he fared poorly, many a soldier survived on rice and beans while his mount enjoyed hay. Conversations in the barracks often turned to which diet was better.

While in garrison the quality of army food depended upon the talent and imagination of the men who were assigned bake house and kitchen duty. In some cases soldiers remarked that travel rations were preferable to what was produced by some of their comrades in garrison. Travel rations consisted of salted beef or pork, coffee, sugar, and whatever could be procured from nature's bounty. J. Walker, assistant surgeon at Fort Scott, noted in his September 30, 1846 quarterly report that "Both COS [companies], particularly the dragoons had previous to their arrival here living on commissary rations, here they indulged in a variety of vegetables and watermelons, musk melons, green apples &C &C [etc] to an unlimited extent. The health of the command is improving." Men in garrison were given a wider variety of items that made for healthier soldiers.

In 1841, the general regulations for the army of the United States called for the proper feeding of soldiers. This included bread and soup as the major components of the soldier's diet. This was of course for the ease of cooking. With so many men to feed at one time, soups and stews were easy to fix in mass quantities and could be kept warm long

enough to ensure that men received a hot meal. Bread could also be baked in large quantities, enough to feed an entire battalion in a single sitting. There's something about hot bread that tastes special but it was believed to hold no nutritional value, especially since the yeast and rising agents needed to settle and cool to ensure proper digestion. Vegetables, sometimes scarce, were cooked very slowly and with great care to ensure that they were

softened. Soft vegetables were easier to chew given the lack of dental hygiene in the nineteenth century. Army regulations stipulated that a man needed to have two opposing teeth in good working order to tear apart the paper that encased the powder for his musket. They also came in handy for eating steak.

Clearly, the health and well-being of the soldier on the trail and in garrison depended on having nutritious food. Beef was a key component—in many ways their health food. It delivered protein, essential fatty acids, and nutrients that weren't even discovered until the twentieth century. Whether he ate his beef salted, dried and salted, boiled and salted, baked and salted, or broiled and salted, the average soldier preferred any form of beef to an empty stomach. Dried and salted beef and salt pork were easy to transport in a soldier's haversack along with his tobacco, hardtack, coffee, lucifers (matches), writing paper and pencil, tintypes in union or gutta percha (rubber which was hardened to be durable) cases, and other items to make his weary, bloodied feet seem less painful on the long march in a time of war. On January 2, 1863, Captain Porter remarked that his "company was detailed to take charge of a herd of Government cattle and proceeded to Fayetteville, the county seat of Washington County, Ark." The need for beef saw no end, even in times of war.

The recipes here reflect the needs of the army in the west. Many of these can be easily replicated for today's healthy tastes and scaled down to feed your modern army at home, in front of the campfire or on the trail!

Military Recipes

Army life was built around the bugle call. It woke men in the morning, guided posting of the colors, and told men when to eat, work, and sleep. The army also understood that food, one of the soldier's few enjoyments, needed to be regimented. Each soldier in garrison received a daily ration of bread, salt pork or beef, vegetables if available, and other items provided by the army though the Quartermaster. These rations were supposed to last a man for an entire month. Once a soldier's rations ran out he would be expected to procure supplies for himself from the post sutler. The sutler on any military post sold everything from fabric to foodstuffs and had a monopoly over the sale of goods not provided to soldiers by the Quartermaster supply. Any soldier could purchase goods against his meager salary. Nuts, fruits, vegetables, spices, grains, sugars, meats, wild game, cheese, crackers, grits, olive oil, oysters in cans and jars, pickles, licorice, rock candy, and liquor were all to be found at the sutler's store on post.

KITCHEN PHILOSOPHY

*R*emember that beans, badly boiled, kill more than bullets; and fat is more fatal than powder. In cooking, more than anything else in the world, always make haste slowly. One hour too much is vastly better than five minutes too little, with rare exceptions. A big fire scorches your soup, burns your face, and crisps your temper. Skim, simmer, and scour are the true secrets of cooking.

—THE UNITED STATES ARMY MANUAL FOR COOKS, 1883

No soldier's day would be complete without coffee. Prior to the American Civil War coffee was sold green and roasting was the duty of the purchaser. The army took care to ensure that cooks, both in garrison and on the march, knew how to properly roast and prepare coffee. Like any well-oiled machine, the army even suggested certain kinds of coffees for soldiers based on where they were stationed and their access to rations.

Rio coffee is generally provided for the use of troops at eastern stations, while on the Pacific coast Central American is preferred, both being good strong coffees. Coffee should be regular in grain (so as to roast evenly) and uniform in color. All coffee improves in flavor by age.

—*THE UNITED STATES ARMY*
MANUAL FOR COOKS, 1886

TO PREPARE COFFEE, NO. 1

Coffee is best when made from the freshly roasted berry. To one pound of coffee, roasted and ground, add ten quarts of boiling water in some convenient vessel, cover the vessel closely to prevent escape of aroma, and place it in a vessel of boiling water, being careful not to let it rest on the bottom of the outer vessel. Boil fifteen minutes. The water in which the coffee is mixed does not boil but remains at a temperature a few degrees below the boiling point. It can be cleared by pour-bagging [straining] it through a piece of flannel or a hair sieve. This will make a strong infusion.

TO PREPARE COFFEE, NO. 2

The vessel should be clean and the water fresh and clear. Fill the vessel with the necessary quantity of water and put it over a brisk fire. When it comes to a boil, stir in the coffee previously moistened with warm (not hot) water. Cover closely; let it boil up for two minutes, stirring from the sides and top as it boils up. Exercise great care that the coffee does not boil over. To clear it, remove it from the fire and dash over the surface a cup of cold fresh water; cover closely and set it on the back of the stove to keep warm but not to boil.

The presence of wormholes in coffee should not occasion its rejection unless it is of inferior quality and strength, since they generally indicate age, weigh nothing, and disappear when the coffee is ground. All coffees should be well cleaned before being roasted.

—ARMY MANUAL FOR COOKS, 1886

REMARKS ON MEAT

Good, fresh beef presents the following characteristics: The lean, when freshly cut, is of a bright red color, easily compressed and elastic, the grain fine and interspersed with fat. The fat is firm and of a yellowish-white color; the suet firm and perfectly white. If beef is of inferior quality the lean is coarse, tough, and inelastic, and of a dull purplish color; the fat is scanty, yellow, and moist.

—MANUAL FOR ARMY COOKS, 1883, 1896

POUNDED BEEF

Cut the lean meat from a shin of beef weighing ten pounds. Break up bone and lay in the bottom of the kettle. Place meat on bones, cover with cold water, and let it slowly come to a boil, removing scum as it rises. Peel two turnips and two onions, scrape one carrot, and place with beef after the broth is skimmed. (If available, put in a half cup of green sweet herbs and parsley.) Also add one level teaspoonful of salt. Cover kettle closely and boil slowly for six hours. At the end of the six hours take up meat, fat, and gristle, remove all bone, put into a colander, and rub through with a potato masher. Season highly and press firmly into a tin or earthen mold. Strain broth left and save it for soup, using enough to moisten meat in mold. After pressing beef into mold and moistening with broth, put a weight on to keep it down and put away to cool. When beef is quite cold, turn out of mold and cut into thin slices.

BOILED SALT BEEF

Salt beef before being cooked should be well washed, and then, when practicable, soaked in cold water for twenty-four hours, changing the water three times.

The meat should be placed in a pot of cold water and made to boil quickly. As soon as the water boils, the meat must be taken out and the water replaced with fresh cold water; boil it according to quality and size of pieces until thoroughly cooked.

BAKED SALT BEEF

Wash the meat as above, make a paste of flour and water, cover the meat with it, and bake in a slow oven twenty minutes for every pound of meat.

❧

STEWED SALT BEEF

Wash the meat as above, and cut into slices; have some chopped greens or soak desiccated mixed vegetables, and put them with the meat and a little water in a stew pan; season, and stew gently for two hours.

With hundreds of hungry mouths to feed on post and on the patrol up and down the Indian frontier line, the army needed beef—dried, salted, and on the hoof. Salted and dried beef could be placed in ration bags and carried in a man's haversack, an oversized purse, that contained food and personal items that the soldier could easily access while on the trail, on horseback, or while gathered around the glow of a nighttime campfire.

The recipes that follow are to be found in the cooking guides that were provided to soldiers at Fort Laramie, Wyoming. Providing detailed instructions did not always yield fare that was pleasing to all soldiers. One needed imagination and patience to survive on a western post like Fort Laramie.

Irish Stew

- 16 ½ pounds of meat
- 16 pounds of potatoes
- 4 pounds of onions
- 6 ounces salt
- 1 ounce pepper
- ½ pound flour

Serves around 22 men

Cut the meat away from the bone, and then into pieces of ¼ pound each; if a loin or neck of mutton, cut into chops; if a shoulder, disjoint it, and cut the blade bone into 4 pieces; if a leg, cut the meat into slices ¾-inch thick; rub the meat with the salt, pepper, and flour, and place it in the boiler with some fat, brown it on both sides, then add the onions whole, and then the potatoes, and enough water to cover the potatoes; stew gently for 2 hours; keep the fire down during the cooking and the boiler well covered.

Buffalo Tongue

- Buffalo tongue
- 1 teaspoon peppercorns
- Dash of salt
- ¼ cup grated onion
- 2 bay leaves

Buffalo tongue recipes also appear in earlier time periods and run through the cattle trade era in Kansas history.

Boil meat with the peppercorns, salt, onion and bay leaves for 2 hours. Serve sliced thin, either hot or cold.

The army was frugal, practical, and resourceful. On the plains and prairies of the West when beef was not available to feed hungry men, buffalo was seen as a viable source of protein for the soldier's diet. They also would hunt smaller game such as deer, elk, pronghorn antelope, pheasant, and prairie chickens. This allowed the army to stretch rations and provide for the men in lean times when supplies were not forthcoming.

Fort Laramie Slumgullion

- Stew meat
- Potatoes
- Turnips
- Onions
- Any additional foraged vegetables
- Pepper and salt
- Water

Parboil the meat until tender. Add to boiling pot vegetables cut into pieces. Add water to sufficiently cover ingredients. Pepper and salt mixture and then boil until done, usually about 1 hour.

Texacus

This recipe originated in Mexico and was brought back to America by those soldiers that had fought in the Mexican War. This version of the recipe is said to have come from a man who was held as a prisoner of war during the conflict.

- 1 pound ground beef
- 1 medium onion, chopped
- 1 cup rice, raw and uncooked
- Salt and pepper to taste
- ½ teaspoon of thyme (important)
- 1 medium head of cabbage
- 2 cups water

Mix together beef, onion, rice, thyme, salt, and pepper. Carefully take outside cabbage leaves off head and put in hot water to soften them, then wrap large spoonfuls of the beef mixture in leaves and secure with toothpicks, and place in large kettle to boil; put a plate on top to hold the cabbage and keep secure. If you want, put them in a pressure cooker for about 15 to 20 minutes.

Spanish Steak

- 2 pounds round steak
- 6 red chilies
- 2 cloves
- 1 tablespoon flour
- A little garlic, thyme, and dripping

Seed the chilies and cover with boiling water. Soak until tender and then scrape the pulp into water. Cut steak into small pieces, fry brown in hot dripping or butter; add flour and brown it. Cover with the chilies water and add garlic and thyme. Simmer until the meat is tender and the gravy is of the right consistency.

The Spanish influence in army cooking in the West extended beyond the Mexican War. The *United States Army Manual for Cooks* includes an entire section devoted to Spanish recipes that undoubtedly gave the men some variety in their otherwise standard diets of beans and rice.

Hardtack (Hardcrackers)

- 4–5 cups flour
- 2 cups water
- Salt

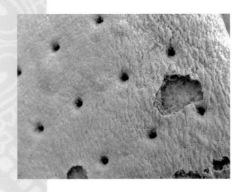

Knead flour, water, and salt; roll out on greased pan; cut into 15 pieces; pierce each piece with 16 holes. Bake for 30 minutes at 425 degrees (15 minutes on each side). Reduce temperature to 200 degrees and bake until all moisture is removed from the crackers (this will take 8 to 24 hours).

If you value your teeth make sure that you soak your hardtack cracker in camp coffee or water or soften it in hot broth, tea, or with morning mush.

—ANONYMOUS JOURNAL ENTRY

This was good advice. During the Civil War many a soldier lost a good tooth to improperly baked hardtack. Hardtack was one of the most portable foods that could be rationed to men on the march. Lightweight, economical, and easy to pack and transport, the army mastered the art of hardtack.

Army Bread Recipe

- 9 cups water
- 2 tablespoons powdered yeast
- 11–13 cups unsifted flour
- 2 tablespoons salt
- Lard

Yields approximately eight 18-ounce loaves

Pour 4 cups lukewarm water into a bowl. Dissolve 2 tablespoons yeast, and then mix in 4 cups unsifted flour. Let bowl sit covered with a towel in a warm place for 1 hour. Add 5 more cups lukewarm water, salt, and 7 to 9 cups flour until doughy consistency is reached. Mix well, kneading in bowl. Cover and set aside in a warm place to rise. After rising, knead dough on a flat, lightly-floured surface. Return to bowl, coat surface with lard, and set aside for 1 hour. Then knead dough lightly, cut into twenty-ounce loaves. Place into greased pans, coating loaves again lightly with lard. Cover and let rise. When sufficiently risen, place pans in oven preheated to 400 degrees and bake 30 to 45 minutes or until golden brown.

This recipe is still used today at many of the former western forts that are now state and national parks where living history interpreters recreate the bake house of the nineteenth century to help educate visitors about army life. Herbs and other spices and additives such as molasses could be added to bread to give it flavor and extend shelf life. At Fort Scott National Historic Site soldiers that have bake house duty often add thyme, basil, parsley, and other herbs that could have been grown on post or ordered through the sutler (provisioner) to their bread.

One of the main keys to army cooking was quantity. Soups, stews, broths, and other dishes that could be cooked in large quantity were preferable for army cooks. One-pot meals were best, as they only required the cook to throw all ingredients in with less fuss. Imagination was the most important ingredient that an army cook could add to any dish, especially during times of the year when vegetables were in short supply.

While the modern military has soldiers that are specifically assigned to cook for their troops, the nineteenth-century army did not have such a system. Cooks and bakers in the army worked on a rotating schedule. The quality of the meals served to the men depended on the individual cooking skills of the man assigned to mess hall or bake house duty.

Dried Bean Soup (from Stock)

- 2 quarts dried beans
- 2 pounds bacon
- 1 gallon stock
- Salt and pepper to taste

Wash the beans and soak them overnight. In the morning drain the water off and cover them again with boiling water; add the bacon and boil gently 2 hours or more; then add the stock. Press the beans through a sieve, return them to the soup kettle, and bring to a boil; add salt and pepper, and serve with toasted bread.

Bombshells

- 16 ½ pounds meat
- 1 pound onions
- 3 ounces salt
- 6 pounds flour
- 1 ounce pepper
- Sweet herbs
- Water

Serves 22 men

Cut all the meat from the bone and sinews, reserving 1½ pounds of fat for the paste. Chop up the meat like sausage meat with the onions and herbs shred fine; season with one-half the salt and pepper. (In India it is the custom to mix spices, capsicums, fruit, etc., with the meat.)

Make the paste as follows: Place the flour on a table, make a hole with your hand in the center, in which place the chopped fat and the remaining salt and pepper, then put some water in the hole; gradually stir the flour into it until it is all moistened and forms a stiff paste; work and roll it well for 2 minutes; let it remain as a ball for 10 minutes, then roll it out to the thickness required.

Have some very clean pudding cloths ready; their size must depend on the size of the shell. Before being used, the cloth should be dipped into boiling water, wrung out, and some flour dusted over the part the pudding will occupy. This prevents the pudding from sticking to the cloth. Divide the paste according to the size, for either 12- or 32-pounders; form it into a ball, and roll it out round; divide the chopped meat and place it in the paste; add a little water; gather it round like a dumpling; bring the cloth around it, and tie it tightly, and boil according to size: a 12-pounder, for one person, 1¾ hours; 32-pounder, for 2–2½ hours.* Some salt should be put into the water the puddings are boiled in. This applies to all boiled puddings or dumplings made with flour and dripping suet.

The bones and cuttings must be made into a gravy, and served separately.

*The terms 12- and 32-pounder refer to two types of nineteenth-century artillery pieces, the 12-pound field gun and the 32-pound siege gun. Military life and its unique jargon influenced the way in which army cooks spoke of their food. A 12-pounder shell was approximately 4 ½-inches in diameter, a 32-pounder shell approximately 8 inches.

Fricassee of Beef

- ½ pound of steak or sirloin
- Handful of parsley
- 1 medium-sized onion
- Butter
- Beef broth
- Salt and pepper
- 2 egg yolks
- 1 teaspoon vinegar
- Wine for flavor
- Garlic clove

Cut your beef into very thin slices. Shred parsley very small. Cut an onion into 4 pieces. Put all into a stew pan with a piece of butter and some strong broth. Season to taste with salt and pepper. Simmer gently for 15 minutes. Now, mix in quickly and well 2 yolks of eggs and a spoonful of vinegar. A small glass of wine will improve the flavor. Heat your serving bowl after you rub it with garlic clove.

Why the Prairie

Early explorers had never seen anything like the expanse of grass that stretched beyond the forests of the East. It was like discovering an inland sea that started in Indiana and Illinois and splashed up against the Rocky Mountains's Front Range. It certainly looked like an ocean, with swells of green rippling before the wind as it moved across tall-stemmed grasses.

The Europeans knew forests and deserts but had no name for grasslands as big as the sky itself. So the French *voyageurs* called it "prairie." It meant lawn. They should have called it pasture. What they at first described as a world of "nothing" was soon filled with a brown mass of steaming, snorting, rutting, wallowing beasts moving like flowing molasses across the landscape. Bison, in what may be the largest herd of any single species in history, used the huge grassland as their pasture. They grazed as they roamed north and south.

Their migration holds one key to understanding why only grasses grow here. It took five days for some herds to pass over a single patch of ground. After they were gone, having munched every living thing in their path down to bare earth, it looked as though nothing would grow again. And yet the shoots would come up the next year in mid-April when the rains collected in prairie potholes.

It turns out that beneath the surface, the plant's roots descended five, ten, even fifteen and twenty feet into the soil. They had learned to survive the buffalo's scorched earth devastation by going underground. Roots seemed long enough to be upside-down trees in the soil.

So when buffalo devoured the prairie, or when fire struck a similar blow, or when drought caused everything on the surface to wither, the grasses sought refuge in the soil. When the danger had passed, a green shoot would emerge to collect the solar power called photosynthesis that turned carbon dioxide into sugar and cranked up the living organism once again. The grasses survived nature's protective elements but trees could not. Grass was assured a dominant place in the Tallgrass prairie.

Today, Tallgrass cattle try to follow the buffalo's pattern. We call it intensive rotational grazing. Herds are kept on measured paddocks in the pasture until they have eaten all the grass and legumes down to the point where it looks like a mown lawn, but not far enough to signal to the plant the apocalypse that accompanied the buffalo. We leave enough plant stem to encourage the grass to grow its leaves back rather than retreat into the soil for protection. Intensive grazing actually helps maintain the pasture and keeps the grass healthy.

Without grass there can be no grass-fed cattle. It wasn't a lack of grass that killed off the bison. Buffalo hunters did that.

chapter 3

Moving West

The hospitality of a prairie home and hearth is one of the most enduring legacies of westward settlement. Food has always been at the core of prairie life: when prairie travelers stopped for the night it was taken for granted that they would be treated to supper; people used food to give thanks for help in raising a barn, or to console a family after the death of a loved one. Maybe they appreciated a good meal more in those days, considering how hard food was to get—hunting it was not easy and judging from early travel narratives, growing it required a preacher's faith and a gambler's acceptance of the game of chance.

We now encountered a great deal of wet weather; in fact this region is famous for cold protracted rains of two or three days' duration. Storms of hail-stones larger than hen's eggs are not uncommon, frequently accompanied by the most tremendous hurricanes. The violence of the wind is sometimes so great that, as I have heard, two road-wagons were once capsized by one of these terrible thunder-gusts; the rain, at the same time, floating the plain to the depth of several inches. In short, I doubt if there is any known region out of the tropics, that can 'head' the great prairies in 'getting up' thunder-storms, combining so many of the elements of the awful and sublime.

—Josiah Gregg

Homes on the prairie were simple and reflected the ability of the average family to adapt to their surroundings and environment, much like the American Indian. Emma Kreuter, another Kansas pioneer, observed, "Many lived in dugouts; with beds made by driving forked poles in the ground for posts and long slender pieces hewn off for the side ends and sates; and with fire places in the back and for warmth to cook on. Our bread consisted mostly of hoe cake." The average family on the prairie found that, if they changed their way of thinking, nature could provide the bounty a family needed to survive. "Out on the prairie, sod houses were numerous. They were made by turning the sod with a breaking plow three or four inches thick and twelve to fourteen in width and length . . . the floors were of dirt, packed hard. A door or two and windows with cloth hung over them. They were quite comfortable . . . they burned buffalo or cow chips, or drove miles for cord wood or coal."

While many families were materially less wealthy than by today's standards, they considered themselves to be rich in creativity and spirit and depended on the prairie to provide them with physical and spiritual comforts. The buffalo, wild and free ranging, was a source of wonder to many prairie families from the East unaccustomed to such massive animals. The family of Emily Biggs found multiple uses for the buffalo. "Coats and caps and mittens and leggings were often made of this leather . . . buffalo tallow candles furnished their light. Buffalo meat, fresh or cured, was their staple article of diet," Emily wrote. For a time, buffalo robes and bones provided a family with quick cash as eastern tastes demanded the hides of the animals for decoration.

Prairie Settlers' Recipes

Cookbooks from the nineteenth century often gave prairie women helpful hints, menu planning ideas for weekly meals, special suppers for entertaining, and quick and easy lunches that could be made on laundry days. Many ideas regarding beef and its uses and cooking methods are to be found in cookbooks like the *Kansas Home Cook Book*, a collection of recipes from the pioneer women of Kansas. Often their advice could be confusing, as in these two examples:

When roasting beef do not put any water in the pan. Rub the meat with salt and pepper, and put it in a slow oven. The juice of the meat will be sufficient to baste it.

All kinds of meats can be cooked more quickly by adding to the water a little vinegar or lemon juice. The acid will make a saving of fuel and time.

However a woman on the homestead chose to cook her cuts of meat, one thing is certain: Meat was quickly becoming the mainstay of the American diet. And beef, especially during the post-Civil War years, was the meat of choice for many Americans. The number of meat recipes, the varieties of meat dishes, and the myriad ways to cook beef all point to the growth in the beef trade. Even the homesteading family desired the rich, full-bodied flavor and texture of beef, but when it was in short supply rabbit, venison, elk, and buffalo were all on the menu. Cooking the beef properly—not over- or under-spicing—was paramount to being a proper hostess.

REMARKS ON MEAT

As meat is the most costly and extravagant of all articles of food, it behooves the housewife to save all leftovers and work them over into other dishes. The so-called inferior pieces—not inferior because they contain less nourishment, but inferior because the demand for such meat is less—should be used for all dishes that are chopped before cooking, as Hamburg steaks, curry balls, kibbee, or for stews, ragouts, pot roasts, and various dishes where a sauce is used to hide the inferiority and ugliness of the dish. We have no occasion here to spend money on good looks.

—KANSAS HOME COOK BOOK, 1886

ROAST BEEF

The best parts for roasting are the sirloin and rib pieces. When roasted in an oven, dash a cup of boiling water over the meat; this checks the escape of the juices. Baste frequently with salt and water and the drippings. Allow about a quarter of an hour to a pound if you like the beef rare, more if you prefer it done. For gravy, remove the beef to a dish, skim the drippings, add a cup of boiling water, and a teaspoon of flour stirred in cold water. Salt and pepper to taste. Serve with mustard or scraped horseradish.

SPICED BEEF

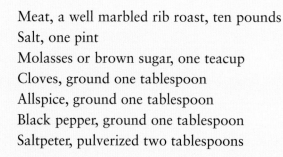

Meat, a well marbled rib roast, ten pounds
Salt, one pint
Molasses or brown sugar, one teacup
Cloves, ground one tablespoon
Allspice, ground one tablespoon
Black pepper, ground one tablespoon
Saltpeter, pulverized two tablespoons

Rub the beef with this mixture and put it into an earthen jar, turning and rubbing it twice a day for a week. Wash off the spices, and put it in a pot of boiling water to cook slowly for five hours over a slow fire. When done, press under a heavy weight until cold.

ROAST BEEF NO. 2

The nicest piece for roasting is the rib. Two ribs of fine beef is a piece large enough for a family of eight or ten. The lean of beef should always appear of a bright red before it is cooked and the fat of a very light cream color.

Season beef with salt and place it in a roaster before a clear, bright fire. Do not set it too close at first. As to the time for roasting, that must be left to the judgment of the cook and the taste of those who eat it. If it is preferred quite rare, an hour and a half or two hours will cook two ribs sufficiently, but if it is to be better done, it must be cooked a proportionally longer time. Whilst the beef is roasting, baste it frequently with its own gravy. When nearly done, dredge flour lightly over it so as to brown it. When the meat is taken out, skim off the fat on the top of the gravy and pour the remainder in the pan; add a little flour, salt to taste, and some water; give it one boil, and serve it in a small tureen or gravy boat.

In cold weather the plates should be warmed just before the dinner is served. Or, a small chafing dish placed under each plate.

BEEF STEAKS

Scrape some fine sirloin steaks, wipe them with a clean cloth, heat the bars of your gridiron, grease them, and put your steaks over clear coals. Turn them frequently by placing a dish over them, and then quickly turn them, holding the dish in one hand and the gridiron in the other. In this manner you will preserve the gravy. When done, season them with pepper and salt; baste them well with butter, and add two tablespoonfuls of water, with a little salt. Send them to the table hot.

FRIED BEEF STEAK

Season your steaks with salt and pepper, and fry them in hot lard. When done, dish them, add a little flour to the fat they were fried in, pour in a little water, and season with pepper and salt to taste; give the gravy one boil and pour it over.

❧

SMOTHERED STEAK

Take one dozen large onions, boil them in very little water until they are tender. Pound and wash a beef steak, season it with pepper and salt, put it in a pan with some hot beef dripping, and fry it until it is done. Take it out; put it on a dish, where it will be kept hot. Then, when the onions are soft, drain and mash them in the pan with the steak gravy, and add pepper and salt to the taste. Put it on the fire and as soon as it is hot, pour it over the steak and serve.

❧

FRENCH STEW, NO. 2

Cut up one pound of beef in small pieces about an inch square, pare and slice six onions; put a layer of the meat and a layer of the onions in a stew pan, with salt and pepper and a little flour alternately and till all is in, and add half a teacup full of water; cover it closely and set it on a slow fire to stew; when about half done, if the gravy seems too thin, add one ounce of butter rolled in flour; but if it should be thick enough, add the butter without the flour.

When tomatoes are in season two tomatoes may be cut in small pieces and stewed with the meat. Cold beef may be cooked in the same manner.

In Kansas, prairie women wrote extensively about the bounty of the land that filled their sod house kitchens with food for the family and any passers-by who may stop seeking comfort. One Kansas woman remarked, "Although our living was very plain, cornbread, meat, mostly prairie chicken, sorghum molasses, etc. we had to go to Clay Center for granulated sugar, beans or rice and some hardware such as nails, etc." Many pioneer families thought themselves to be very fortunate to have a roof over their heads and food on the table. Luxury items were far from the thoughts of most women as necessity was not only the mother of invention, but more important, survival. When beef was either in short supply or too expensive, venison, elk, buffalo, and other wild game were often substituted in many standard recipes.

FRIED RABBIT

Rabbits to fry must be young or parboiled. Cut into joints; soak for an hour in salt and water, dip into beaten egg, then in powdered cracker and fry brown in sweet lard or butter. Serve with onion sauce; garnish with sliced lemon.

BAKED PRAIRIE CHICKEN

Stuff the chicken with a prepared dressing of bread, season with butter, pepper, salt, and summer savory. Bind on the outside thin slices of sweet bacon, and baste often while cooking. Remove the bacon before sending to the table.

SNIPE

Draw each bird nicely, and fill in with a piece of bread and butter, well seasoned with pepper and salt. Fold around each bird a thin piece of pickled pork, fastened with the bill of the bird. Place in a dripping pan, and bake it one half hour basting frequently. Add a little butter to the gravy if necessary, and serve hot.

QUAIL ON TOAST

Each quail should be carefully picked, cut open down the back, and pounded slightly with the steak pounder to break the bones, that they may lie flat on the gridiron. Salt and pepper them, and broil to a nice brown, dipping each piece when cooked in a pan containing melted butter and pepper. Have ready slices of bread, toasted to a light brown and well buttered; also, broken down with a knife to make it tender. Lay a bird on each piece of the toast, and pour the butter in which they were dipped over the whole. Serve at once.

TO COOK AN OLD FOWL

Cut it up, wash well, and put it in a pot with only a tablespoon of water. Cook over a slow fire about three hours. The moisture from the chicken will make sufficient gravy. Spice to taste.

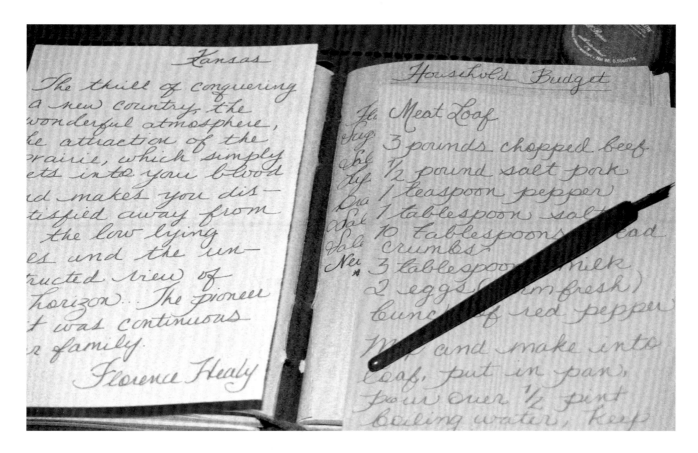

Many housewives kept books in which they clipped recipes from newspapers, wrote down household hints, wrote their own poems and daily reflections, and crafted their own unique recipes for their families. Kitty Hayes Houghton was one such woman. Her notes, ideas on self-improvement, newspaper clippings on important issues, and recipes provide a glimpse into the Flint Hills ranching lifestyle. The following recipes, from Kitty and other pioneer wives, were found on tattered pages in between self-help columns, advertisements for dyspepsia cures, notes on hospitality, and poetry and short stories written by women with much imagination and creativity.

Meat Loaf

- 3 pounds chopped beef
- ½ pound salt pork
- 1 teaspoon pepper
- 1 tablespoon salt
- 10 tablespoons bread crumbs
- 3 tablespoons milk
- 2 eggs
- Bunch of red pepper

Mix and make into loaf, put in pan, pour over ½ pint boiling water, keep water in pan all of the time—bake 2 hours.

Meat Rocks

- 2 pounds flank steak
- 2 tablespoons mustard
- 2 stalks celery
- 2 carrots
- 2 tablespoons flour
- 2 tablespoons fat
- 2 small onions
- 1 cup tomatoes
- 2 medium-sized potatoes
- 1 teaspoon salt
- ¼ of a pepper

Cut steak in 4 pieces a little longer than wide. Spread with 2 tablespoons of mustard. Have your celery and carrots cut in strips rather full. Place in steak, roll up, and fasten with skewers or toothpicks. Roll in seasoned flour and brown in hot fat. Arrange in casserole or baking pan. Add chopped onions and tomatoes. Bake in covered vessel; at the end of the first 30 minutes add peeled potatoes and a little water. Let bake in all about 1 hour and 15 minutes. Thicken gravy before serving.

Flank Steak

- Flank steak
- Mustard
- Dill pickles
- Onion
- Strips of bacon
- Salt and pepper
- 1 egg, beaten
- Cracker or bread crumbs

Get flank steak spread with prepared mustard. Slice dill pickle the long way, slice onion in thin strips.

Put the pickle, onion, bacon, salt and pepper on the meat, roll and hold together with skewers or toothpick. Roll in beaten egg then in cracker crumbs, sear in hot fat. Add water and bake in oven 1½ or 2 hours.

Mrs. Peaks's Pineapple Cucumber Salad

- 2 tablespoons gelatin
- 1 flat can grated pineapple (half size)
- Juice of 2 lemons
- 1 cucumber about 6 inches long
- ½ cup sugar
- 1 envelope Knox

Serves about 10

Soak gelatin in ½ cup cold water, add to hot fruit juice and make sure sugar has been dissolved. Chop pineapple and cucumber fine. Mix and chill. Serve with mayonnaise.

Beef à-la-Mode

- 1 two-pound round roast
- 1 pint bread crumbs
- 1 small onion, chopped
- 1 ounce butter
- Salt and pepper
- Cloves or allspice to taste

A round of beef is the best for this purpose. With a sharp knife cut incisions in the meat about an inch apart, and within 1 inch of the opposite side, season it with pepper and salt to the size of the piece of meat.

Make a dressing of butter, onion, and bread crumbs, in the proportion of a pint of crumbs, one small onion finely chopped, and an ounce of butter, with pepper and salt to the taste, fill the incisions with the dressing, put the meat in a pot with about a pint of water, and cover tightly. Let simmer 6 or 8 hours.

Some stick in a few cloves, and those who are fond of spice can add allspice. When the meat is done, dish it up and thicken the gravy with a little flour. Let it boil once, serve it. This is excellent when cold.

Of all the enduring images of prairie life and settlements, the town of Walnut Grove and its inhabitants as described by Laura Ingalls Wilder endures in the American imagination. Written in her later years, Wilder's books have a nostalgic quality that makes us all yearn for a return to the life of a child on the prairie, free from life's worries and cares.

The official historic site of the Ingalls family settlement in Kansas is located near Wayside, twelve miles southwest of Independence, Kansas. They lived here for only one year. Today, the site features a small, historically accurate reproduction of the log cabin described by Laura in Little House on the Prairie. In 1970, the owners of the land, Brigadier General and Mrs. William A. Kurtis, moved a one-room schoolhouse alongside the cabin. Wilma Kurtis's mother, Mrs. Bert L. Horton, taught there as a frontier school teacher. Situated in good grazing lands, this area was primed for settlers as it afforded them good water, timber, and grass. The families of Wayside and Independence, Kansas, are proud of their ties to the Ingalls family and produced a cookbook that reflected that idealized bygone era. The following recipes are based on those from the original pioneer families of the area and kitchen-tested for your family and your own prairie table.

Helen's Baked Hash

- 2 ½ cups cooked roast beef
- 2 cups raw potatoes
- Salt and pepper, as desired
- 1 medium-sized onion, chopped

Serves 4

Grind beef and potatoes together so that the moisture from the potatoes is absorbed by the beef. Add salt, pepper, and any other seasonings as desired. Place in a well-greased casserole dish and dot with butter. Bake 45 minutes at 350 degrees or until top is crusty. This is such a good way to use leftover roast beef. It makes a main dish and is it ever tasty.

Lucine's Five-Hour Stew

- 1 ½ pounds cubed, boneless beef stew meat
- 6 carrots, sliced 1-inch thick
- 3 onions, quartered
- 1 cup celery, cut in 1-inch pieces
- 1 can tomatoes, large size
- 3 medium potatoes, diced
- 1 tablespoon salt
- 1 tablespoon sugar
- 3 tablespoons tapioca
- 1 slice fresh bread, cubed

Mix all ingredients together. Place in a large casserole dish. Bring to a boil and remove from heat immediately, then back in oven at 250 degrees for 5 hours.

This is a large recipe and part of it can be frozen. A terrific thing to warm up in a hurry—you are ready for any emergency to feed unexpected guests.

The previous recipes can also be prepared in a Dutch oven. While modern, it is based on the traditional stews of the Old West. A true prairie hostess would always be ready to feed an extra mouth at the table and could accommodate many with very little from her kitchen. This is the true expression of prairie hospitality.

Lynch's Famous Chili

Ben Lynch said you could always tell good chili by the kind of chef's cap the cook wore. It should be the tall kind, he said.

- ½ pound ground suet
- 1 ½ pounds hamburger
- 1 small onion, chopped thin and fine
- 1 medium can red beans
- 1 tablespoon chili powder
- Salt and pepper as desired
- 1–2 cups tomato juice

Render suet in a large skillet. Add hamburger and onion. Cook until meat is nearly done. Add beans; season with chili powder, salt, and pepper. Simmer.

More liquid may be added if necessary. Paprika added will give color.

The art of pioneer cooking is still alive today so long as women and men of the Great Plains honor the legacies left behind by their pioneer ancestors. Judy Tolbert of Sedan, Kansas, keeps this spirit alive each moment she spends in the kitchen. Judy recalls that she "learned the love of cooking from [her] grandmother Maude Dillee. She and grandpa were married in Independence, Kansas, on February 21, 1905. My grandmother was a cook at a restaurant in Caney, Kansas. When she and grandpa married, he was living in the 'Tent City' working in old fields at Peru, Kansas. After their marriage, grandma cooked for the workers. A few years later they moved to Sun City, Kansas, where grandpa became a ranch hand and later the foreman for the Moffitt Ranch. Grandma cooked for the Moffitt family and the ranch hands. She would make doughnuts or cookies in the afternoons and a cooler of cold tea and take it to the fields around four o'clock every afternoon during harvest." The memories connected to cooking—the smell of bread baking, the sound of beef in the skillet, the knife on the cutting board chopping vegetables, the time spent in the kitchen with family—all of these influence today's modern prairie cooks. The recipes that follow came from the kitchen of Maude Dillee and are still cooked today in Judy's modern prairie kitchen.

Liver and Onions

Prairie families wasted very little. Cattle were slaughtered for food parts that we find difficult to consider eating but were commonplace on the prairie dinner table. "When we would butcher a cow, grandma made liver and onions; this is still the only way I will eat it so I generally have to fix it myself. It is never tough, dry, or rubbery. She cooked it in the large iron skillet—which I still have."

- Fresh liver, sliced thin
- Salt and flour for coating
- 1 onion, sliced
- 1-2 cups water

Coat liver with salt and flour. Heat lard in skillet. Brown liver on both sides and turn down burner to simmer. Add a big onion sliced, pour 1 to 2 cups of water. Cover tight with lid and let simmer about 30 minutes. It will make its own gravy.

Apple Dumplings

Dough

- 1 ½ cups flour
- 3 tablespoons butter
- 3 teaspoons baking powder
- Pinch of salt
- ½ cup milk

Filling

- 3 or more apples
- Sugar
- Butter
- Nutmeg

Sauce

- 1 ½ cups brown sugar
- 1 tablespoon flour
- 1 pint boiling water
- 1 tablespoon butter

Mix the dough the same as you would a pie crust and roll out rectangular. Three or more apples cut fine, cover the dough. Sprinkle with sugar, butter, and nutmeg. Roll up like a jellyroll, cut in slices, place in a well-greased cake pan. Cover with sauce and bake half hour or until brown.

Good Brown Stew
(Cooked in the Iron Dutch Oven)

- 1 ½–2 pounds flank meat, cut into 1-inch cubes
- ½ cup flour
- 2 teaspoons salt
- ½ teaspoon pepper
- 3 tablespoons fat (such as bacon grease)
- 1 cup water
- 1 medium onion, sliced
- 4–5 quartered potatoes
- 4–5 carrots, cut in large pieces

Put flour, salt, and pepper in a paper sack; drop meat cubes into sack and shake well, being sure to cover meat well.

Put fat into a Dutch oven. When fat is hot, put cubed meat in and brown on all sides. When meat is browned add water. Place onion over top of meat. Put tight lid on and simmer for 2–2 ½ hours. About a half hour before serving time add potatoes and carrots. A small amount of water may be added if necessary. Put lid back on and continue to simmer until done.

With the bicentennial of our nation's birth, communities large and small found themselves looking to the past. In Breckenridge, Texas, families shared their heritage through food, and produced a commemorative cookbook. These recipes have been handed down through the generations, and are treasured as much as prized family photos.

Chili Stew

- 1 medium onion
- 1 medium bell pepper
- 1–2 pounds ground beef
- ¼ teaspoon thyme
- ½ teaspoon pepper
- ¼ teaspoon garlic salt
- ½ teaspoon chili powder
- 1 fifteen-ounce can pinto beans
- 1 teaspoon salt
- Celery salt or celery seed to taste
- 1 large can tomatoes

Sauté one onion sliced into thin rings and one chopped bell pepper. Add 1–2 pounds of ground beef browned, drain off excess grease. Add rest of ingredients.

Bring to boil and simmer until liquid is mostly absorbed. Good made a day before it is to be served so flavors can blend. Serve with cornbread and salad.

Fresh Mountain Oysters

Rocky Mountain Oysters, sometimes called prairie oysters, are buffalo or bull testicles. They are a staple at many western cook-off competitions and are considered a delicacy. One author of a similar recipe for mountain oysters noted: "This is another food that my mother prepared. These are also called calf fries; if you do not know what they are—call me!"

- Mountain oysters
- Seasoning to taste
- Cracker crumbs or flour for coating

Slice the oysters in half. Season as desired. Roll in cracker crumbs or just flour them. Drop in hot grease; cook until golden brown.

Barbecue Style Meatloaf

- 1 ½ pounds ground beef
- 1 onion finely chopped
- 1 ½ teaspoons salt
- 1 can tomato sauce
- 3 tablespoons vinegar
- 2 tablespoons prepared mustard
- 1 cup fresh bread crumbs
- 1 beaten egg
- ¼ teaspoon pepper
- ½ cup water
- 3 tablespoons brown sugar
- 2 teaspoons Worcestershire sauce

Mix beef, bread crumbs, onion, egg, salt, pepper, and ½ can tomato sauce. Form into loaf and place in shallow pan (about 7 × 10). Combine rest of the ingredients and sauce and pour over loaf. Bake at 350 degrees for 1 hour and 15 minutes, basting occasionally.

Beef Jerky

- Flank steak
- Liquid hickory smoke
- Round tooth picks

Trim all the fat off the meat. Cut into strips ¼-inch thick by ½-inch wide and 3 to 6 inches long. Place in a bowl and soak overnight with liquid hickory smoke or for 24 hours. Place round tooth picks into one end of the strips and hang on top rack of oven. Set oven at 130 degrees (not over 140 degrees). Crack oven door about one inch. Leave in oven 10 to 12 hours depending on the thickness of the meat. Remove from oven. Remove toothpicks, let cool for 2 or 3 hours and put in plastic bag or covered jars.

Shannon, K.T. [Kansas Territory], May 18, 1856
I find my washing and some of my work a full
match for me, but have not been laid by but
one a few day since I got over the ague. We
should admire to have you visit us, and eat
some of our new fashioned peas or Osage
plumbs as they are called. We find them plenti-
full and as good as string beans or esparigus
by the first of May. I think you would be
enraptured with the splendid wild flowers, as
well as the country and if it becomes a free
state, and our city worthy of you, we shall
some day have you for a neighbor. But what
you gain there will not more than balance the
novelty, and excitement of our new pioneer
life which is not so despisable after all. I assure
you we have our joys as well as sorrows.

—ELLEN D. GOODNOW

Women are the unsung heroines of the prairie, just as important to its survival as were the railroad and the cattle trade. Ellen D. Goodnow was one of a handful of resolute women who made the trek to Kansas Territory after the Kansas-Nebraska Act opened to settlement in 1854. Leaving all that she had known and admired of eastern life behind her, Ellen followed her husband in the endeavor to make Kansas more than a free state—she hoped it would become her home in the truest sense of the word. For eastern women the desire to replicate their lives of comfort and plenty in the East was a difficult task in the rough and tumble West. The song "Sweet Betsy from Pike" speaks of cholera,

hard work, and despair, and the eventual triumph over adversity and victory for those that stayed the course. In reality, sickness, starvation, the elements, attack, and plain bad luck made lonely trails and picturesque hilltops the final resting places for many that ventured westward. There was, however, always hope of better times to come, the glue that held families and the communities together. Soon, many once tranquil prairie towns would be filled with the noise, hustle, and bustle of a new commodity that would change the economy and diet of the nation—cattle!

The Magic of Grass

Take a walk across the earth and you'll find grasses covering almost one-third of it. When you reach the United States, you'll be knee-high in green and gold fully half the time.

Plants in the grass family keep us alive with wheat, rye, corn, rice, oats, barley, sorghum, and millet. Before they bear their fruit of grain, the leafy parts are eaten by cows and other ruminants. They are called ruminants because they have developed a stomach of four chambers to digest parts of the grass plant that we humans can't. The most important chamber is the rumen, a large cooking vat filled with bacteria specially designed for the job of breaking down the cellulose in the grass and extracting the nutrition.

What a marvelous natural partnership. The sun nourishes the grass that is eaten by cows, transforming solar energy into protein for our consumption. The animals, like good gardeners, maintain the grass crop by trimming it periodically, like mowing the lawn. That encourages the leaves to keep growing back, again and again. In return, the cows leave behind those cute little patties of waste to fertilize next year's grasses.

It took some time for this grass factory to evolve. Like so many things, grasses are thought to have originated in Africa and then, with their seeds carried by the winds, they spread to every continent. If you put yourself in the role of Great Designer, measuring the climate, the moisture, and the soil of various parts of the world, you'd naturally come to grasses as the perfect complement to rain forests, deserts, and mountains.

Somewhere between one hundred million and two hundred million years ago gigantic tectonic forces pulled the super-continent of Pangaea apart. The growing pains left an enormous 3,000-mile-long stretch mark called the Great Rift Valley down what we now call East Africa. The ripping action also created a mountain range in the Ethiopian Highlands. As any good meteorologist could predict, the mountains blocked the rains blowing in from the west and left a rain shadow on the eastern side. Shadow is a good word for it. Since the clouds had dropped their moisture in the mountains, it took a while to build the moisture up again, and since the weather systems were moving all the time, all of East Africa became drier. The rain forest vanished and grasslands appeared. If you notice a similarity between East Africa and the Great Plains between the eastern slope of the Rocky Mountains and the eastern deciduous forests, give yourself a high-five.

What happened next would change life on earth. The intense equatorial sun favored a new type of grass known as Carbon-4 or the C-4 plant. They developed sturdy stems that enabled them to reach above other plants to get even more sunlight. This gave birth to a more powerful solar engine that changed sunlight and carbon dioxide into sugars. In most grasses, the plant's photosynthesis happens at the upper surface. But in C-4 plants, carbon dioxide concentrates around sheath cells deeper in the plant. Those hardy stalks act like solar tubes to funnel the sunlight down to the sheath cells. It's like a nuclear-powered turbine that manufactures sugars and growth much faster than other grasses. In East Africa, the C-4 giants thrived, creating a food source more abundant than any other on earth.

There was one drawback. The stems were tough and difficult to digest for most animals. And that's where the marvel of evolution went to work. Grazing forest animals pulled a fast one on the hard-to-eat grasses. They chewed them twice, literally pumping those that weren't fully digested up from their stomach onto their molars, grinding them all over again. Hence, the phrase "chewing their cud."

After the second chewing, the remaining contents move into the other chambers, which exist just for the tough grasses. There, microbes attack the cellulose and allow the sugars and vitamins to escape.

What a remarkable symbiotic relationship. The result is nature's perfect equation of supply and demand: grass plus cow equals one of the most healthful foods available, ideally suited for *Homo sapiens*. Why? Because we evolved on a diet of wild game, nuts, and roots. We didn't eat the grass because we couldn't break it down. But we ate the animal that transformed sun, carbon dioxide, and grass into protein. Indeed, it was a marriage made in heaven.

Why did we get a divorce? More, as you read on.

chapter 4

The Cowboy Table on the Trail

THE DYING COWBOY

Oh, bury me not on the lone prairie,

Where the wild coyote will howl o'er me,

And the rattlesnake coiling there o'er me.

Oh, bury me not on the lone prairie.

"Oh, bury me not" and his voice failed there;

But they listened not to his dying prayer;

In a narrow grave just six by three

They laid him there on the lone prairie.

Where the dewdrops fall and the butterfly rest,

The wild rose bloom on the prairie's crest;

Where the coyotes howl and the wind blows free,

They buried him there on the lone prairie.

—MYRA HULL, FROM "COWBOY BALLADS," *KSHS QUARTERLY*, FEBRUARY 1939 (VOL. 8, NO. 1), PAGE 47

Solitary men on horseback, lines of cattle as long as the eye can see against the horizon, the soft lowing of cattle as they move along the trail, the smell of bacon and potatoes in old cookie's skillet over the fire—these are among the most enduring images of the cattle trail in the American West. Reproduced in books, magazines, newspapers, and eventually on the silver screen, cowboys were one of the icons of American history and the cattle drive was their stage.

Born out of the need to supply fresh beef to the hungry East and United States troopers to the West, the cattle trade faced two major problems—how to move Longhorns from Texas to Chicago and how to make sure they were fat when they got there. The solution would take superhuman feats of endurance and encountering danger the likes of which would thrill dime novel readers and movie-goers for decades. It would forever brand the image of the cowboy into America's psyche. From a Texas perspective, all you had to do was point north and yell, "Move 'em out!" But wranglers soon realized it was quicker if they followed a trail. It didn't take long for names to appear like Shawnee, Goodnight-Loving, Chisholm, and Western—trails that fanned out from San Antonio and Fort Worth, Texas. In addition to moving cattle, they would open up new areas of the West for commerce and trade. From Texas through Indian Territory and into Kansas, the cattle boom was on and the future would be transformed. Towns sprang up seemingly overnight to ship cattle on rail lines east and to cater to the

the cowboy epoch for that part of Kansas. When they took a notion to shoot up a town, it was well for the residents to stay inside to avoid being hit by stray bullets," Mattie wrote. Most cattle towns, regardless of size or impor-tance, suffered the woes of violence fueled by guns, liquor, tempers, youthful arrogance, and wounded pride. Elgin, Kansas, while smaller than many cattle towns, had sixty-six saloons with more gunfights and violence than most of the larger towns rolled into one.

needs of the dusty, rugged cowboy in need of a shave, a hot bath, and a good meal.

Kansas soon found out that cattle were much easier to control than cowboys. Baxter Springs, Caldwell, Elgin, Abilene, Ellsworth, and Dodge City became famous for what accompanied the cattle herds—action. Mattie Huffman, a resident of several Kansas cattle towns, reflected upon the fast pace of life in the cattle trade era. "In 1879, the Santa Fe Railroad was built from Wichita to Wellington. In a short time the railroad went on as far as Caldwell so that Texas cattle could be shipped from the southern state line." When this rail line was extended just a few weeks later, Mattie noted, "The little town of Hunwell grew up over night, and was doing business before the grass in the streets was killed."

Small towns like Hunwell could be quickly overrun with cowboys who were short-tempered and weary of the trail. "At the time Hunwell grew up [it] was

While many loathed the cowboy and his wild ways, many families living in cattle towns and surrounding areas took pity on them because of their wayward lifestyle. Mrs. Emily Biggs was one such prairie wife. According to her daughter, "[She] boarded the cowboys and washed their flannel shirts and wool socks and knit new stockings for them and wrote letters to the girls they left behind them, for the cowboys of that period were much more proficient with a lariat than with a penholder." Emily also used her culinary skills to satisfy the cowboy's yearning for a true home cooked meal after as many as 150 days on the dusty, hot, unforgiving trail. "She gave them real home cooking, too, the pies used wild goose grease for shortening and dried apples for filling."

The chuck wagon is one of the most recognizable symbols of the American West. Developed by Charles Goodnight to solve the problem of feeding men while driving cattle to market, the chuck wagon was for the cowboy home, hearth, pantry, hospital, and social center. When a cowboy threw his bedroll into the back of a chuck wagon he was giving his oath to that ranch to see the drive through. The chuck wagon was the domain of the "cookie," who was responsible for ensuring that the supplies were loaded and the meals cooked while on the trail.

On the rear of each wagon was a "chuck box," which contained everything from cooking utensils, tinware, spices, medicines, and the cookie's own private bottle of whiskey that was used to cure everything from snakebite to intestinal complaints. This was often the only alcohol allowed on the drive. Food on the trail could be meager—beans, rice, coffee, and biscuits. How ironic to have no meat on a trip driving hundreds of cattle to market!

Corn bread, mast-fed bacon, and coffee constitute nine-tenths of their diet; occasionally they have fresh beef and less often they have vegetables of any description. They do their own cooking in the rudest and fewest possible vessels, often not having a single plate or knife and fork other than their pocket knife . . . not forgetting to stow away one or more quarts of the strongest coffee imaginable, without sugar or cream.

—JOSEPH MCCOY, *SKETCHES OF THE CATTLE TRADE OF THE SOUTH WEST*

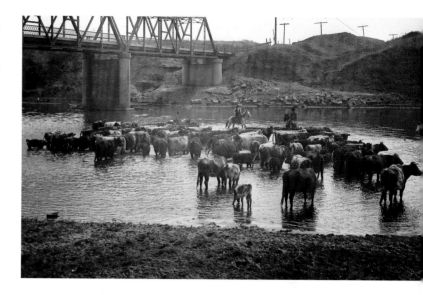

Driving cattle along the trails by day and gathering around the chuck wagon and campfire by night, the lifestyle of the cowboy was wild and free. One can hear the crackling of the fire, see its red-orange glow dotting the night sky, smell the coffee in cookie's giant pot, and hear the sizzle of bacon in the cast iron skillet. The soft lowing of cattle in the herd, men riding along to keep them calm, singing to them in low, soft tones, life on the cattle trail had its beautiful moments.

Ranch and Trail Recipes

In 1909, The Ladies of the First Baptist Church of Amarillo, Texas, published what would become the first cookbook in the history of Amarillo. Situated near the Palo Duro Canyon and the famed JA Ranch run by cattle entrepreneur Charles Goodnight, these recipes were staples on many ranch tables. In the introduction to their work these ladies summed up the cowboy mind best: "We may live without friends, we may live without books, but civilized man can not live without cooks." As we will see later, no self-respecting cowboy would hit the trail with a poor cook!

HAMBURGER

Take about 20 cents' worth (one to two pounds) of ground or chopped meat with plenty of fat; two onions, chopped; two tablespoonfuls chili powder; one cup bread crumbs; salt; make this into a loaf and just before baking pour a can of tomatoes over it; bake about forty-five minutes.

—Mrs. A.S. Tugwell

POT ROAST (OLD STYLE)

This is an old fashioned dish, often cooked in our great-grandmother's time. Take a piece of fresh beef, it must not be too fat; wash it and put it into a pot with barely sufficient water to cover it; set it over a slow fire and after it has stewed an hour salt and pepper it; then stew it slowly until tender, adding a little onion if liked. Do not replenish the water at the last, but let all nearly boil away. When tender all the way through take the meat from the pot and pour the gravy in a bowl. Put a large lump of butter in the bottom of the pot; then dredge the piece of meat with flour to prevent burning and return it to the pot to brown, turning it often to prevent burning. Take the gravy that you have poured from the meat into the bowl and skim off all the fat; pour thick gravy in with the meat and stir in a spoonful of flour wet with a little water; let it boil up to ten to fifteen minutes and pour into gravy dish. Serve both hot, the meat and the platter.

—Mrs. J.F. Tarter

HAMBURG STEAK

Grind lean beef, season with a little onion, pepper, and salt; roll into a flat mound about an inch thick; put it on a very hot griddle, turn it when done, and pour melted butter over it, or you can make into little cakes and broil.

—Mrs. Oakes

CAMP FIRE COFFEE

Heat a pot of cold water to boiling. (Allow to boil only two to three minutes.) Place a cup of ground coffee and an egg in the middle of a piece of cheesecloth and tie the cheesecloth into a sack. Then break the egg in the sack and mix with the coffee by massaging the bag. Drop the sack into the boiling water and cook for four minutes. Add one half cup cold water to settle any grounds. The coffee is absolutely superb.

After the American Civil War the art of roasting coffee underwent a major revolution. With the introduction of a new roasting system, the Arbuckle Brothers gave birth to an American legend. Arbuckle's Coffee was a mainstay in any chuck wagon. A peppermint stick was included in each bag of coffee and was a highly sought-after treat to satisfy the cowboy sweet tooth. Trading cards came in Arbuckle's coffee as well. They covered a variety of topics including music, poetry, and geography as in the example below. Today Arbuckle's is still enjoyed around many a campfire.

Burned beans or poorly cooked meat could make a cowboy ill and miserable. Jack Bailey, traveling the cattle trail from Texas to Kansas in 1868, committed to his journal a most memorable meal on the trail. While moving cattle along the trails it was necessary, at times, to kill those that were sickly, injured, or in some cases too wild to herd well. Bailey wrote "killed a poor yearling yesterday. Meanest beef I ever saw. It was a little grass gutted thing. Had to throw most of it away. I never [saw] as much belly ache as was in camp last night. All very hungry and tired. Had no salt to put on our little yearling. Broiled it. The more we cooked it, the bigger it got. Eat it half done and the consequence was all had the trots all night. Had a big laugh in camp the next morning."

With no medicines to effectively relieve such conditions, cowboys in camp would let such afflictions run their course and get back in the saddle as quickly as possible. While some chuck wagon dishes have hideous names, they were better than the chance taken on an overgrazed yearling with a stomach full of grass.

SONOFABITCH STEW

From the guts of a young calf:
Heart, Liver, Tongue, Tenderloin, Sweetbreads, Marrow gut, Brains

Cube the first five of the meats.
Add them to a hot Dutch oven that has a small amount of lard already melted in the bottom. Brown the meats. Slice the marrow gut, add the marrow gut to the pot; the brains are cooked in a separate pot; add a few tablespoons of flour to thicken them. Add brains to the pot. Add a diced onion, salt, and pepper. Cover in water for 3 hours. Continue to stir and do not allow it to stick.

SQUIRREL CAN STEW

This recipe is from around 1870 and is reprinted exactly the way the cook wrote it down.

Take the bones and trimmings from a sirloin steak, put over a fire after breakfast in three quarts of water, boil steadily until about an hour before dinner, then add two onions, one carrot, three potatoes, all sliced, some parsley cut fine, a red pepper, and salt to taste. This makes a delicious stew. All stews are more palatable seasoned with onions and red pepper using the seeds of the later with care, as they are very strong.

A "squirrel can" was an empty lard can that sat next to the chuck wagon. Cowboys scraped their plates into this can before putting their dishes in the "wreck" pan (dish pan for washing). This was used to keep the camp more sanitary and clean. Cowboys would make remarks and crack jokes about food and coffee tasting as if the cookie had just dipped from the squirrel can. Joking aside, there was a code of conduct that cowboys were to observe with respect to eating and etiquette in camp. Breaking these camp commandments could get you in trouble with cookie and every cowboy knew that cookie was the one man everyone respected and wanted to please. If cookie wasn't happy, no one was happy!

No one eats until Cookie calls.
When Cookie calls, everyone comes to eat.
Hungry cowboys wait for no man.
Cowboys always eat first and talk later, filling the belly is just as important as herding the cattle.
If you're refilling the coffee cup and someone yells "Man at the pot" you must serve others who wish another cup of coffee.
Don't take the last serving unless you know that you are the last man.
The running and saddling of horses near the wagon is not allowed.
When you ride off, do so down wind from the wagon.
Strangers are always welcomed at the wagon; who knows when the kindness of strangers may help you in a time of need.

On occasions when the herd was staying in the same location for a day or two resting, the cook would prepare more elaborate dishes, and if local produce (say eggs or potatoes) could be bought from a nearby homesteader, the menu could include anything. Wild game (antelope, buffalo, wild turkey) also provided a welcome change from bacon and beans.

BERRY COBBLER

Grease a Dutch oven and cover the bottom an inch and a half deep with fresh berries sprinkled with sugar.

To prepare the crust, cut three-fourths cup of butter into two cups of flour. Cut a pinch of salt and a scoop of sugar into the flour. Sprinkle with cold water and mix until it just holds together. Roll out thick and place on top of berries. Put lid on Dutch oven and bake thirty minutes with more heat from the bottom than from the top.

❧

POUNDED STEAK (HAMMERED STEAK)

I learned to love pounded steak from my father and his mother. On shipping mornings I can remember sitting in her kitchen at 4 a.m. listening to my grandfather and three or four other cowboys talk as she pounded steaks, and I remember the smell as she set a platter on the table.

—Jim Hoy, Kansas

Any thin cut of beef will do, although a slice from the round is preferred. Hammer the steak thoroughly on both sides. Dredge it lightly on both sides in salted and peppered flour. In large skillet with the bottom covered in hot oil, fry steaks until golden brown. When done frying steaks, scrape skillet, add a dusting of dredging flour, pour in milk, and simmer for delicious gravy.

BUFFALO EN APPOLAS

Skewer bite-sized pieces of buffalo meat, putting fat between lean. Swab with oil (rendered kidney fat is best), broil over hot coals, and sprinkle with salt and red pepper. The hump of the buffalo is tough and fatty eating but best for high energy needs on the trail and in the saddle. The tender "fleece" meat, on the sides of the hump, is the most juicy and mouthwatering portion of the animal.

Ranch House Pot Roast

This came from a Montana Ranch in the 1890s. It was used by the lady of the house for her family and guests.

- Shortening
- 3–4 pounds of beef roast (chuck works well)
- 2 handfuls of flour
- Salt and pepper to taste
- 2 cups beef broth or water
- 1 medium chopped onion
- 2 cloves of chopped garlic
- 1 bay leaf
- 1 teaspoon sugar
- Pinch of chili powder

Heat a medium amount of shortening in a Dutch oven, over medium-high heat. Season flour with salt and pepper then dredge roast in it. Brown roast in hot fat. Add broth or water, onion, garlic, bay leaf, sugar and chili powder. Cover'n cook in the oven at 325 degrees or on stove over low heat for 2½ hours Then add 2–3 pounds of potatoes cut in half. Cook for another hour or so until potatoes are tender.

Chuck Wagon Bean Soup with Beef

- 1 pound soup beans
- 1 soup bone with meat on it
- 3 diced potatoes
- ¼ cup chopped onions
- 2 teaspoons salt
- ¼ teaspoon pepper
- ¼ teaspoon cloves
- ¼ teaspoon allspice

Soak the beans overnight in water and make sure that the bugs are skimmed off the top in the morning if it was left uncovered. Cook the soup bone with water until the meat is tender. Remove bone. Cut off meat. Cook the beans in the broth, make sure they are soft. Add the meat, potatoes, onion, and seasonings. Simmer until potatoes are soft. Make dough balls from any mix of your choice. Drop in dough balls and boil 5 minutes more.

Frying Pan Supper

- 2 pounds beef
- 1 large onion, in bite-sized pieces
- 1 green pepper or chili pepper, diced large
- 1 clove garlic, crushed
- Salt and pepper to taste
- 1 can of tomatoes
- 1 can of corn or hominy

Brown beef with onion, pepper, garlic, salt, and pepper, then add tomatoes and hominy and cook until well blended. Serve over biscuits or cornbread.

This dish has a South American equivalent called *Carne Molida* that is served in Venezuela with fried bread called *arepas* or over rice or noodles. Venezuela, like the American West, has a cattle ranching tradition that has shaped their history and culture in the region of the nation known as the Llanos.

Pan Fried Steaks

- 1 large steak
- Salt and pepper to taste
- Beef suet
- Butter

Heat a large cast-iron pan on medium-high heat until it is good 'n hot. Then add some rendered beef suet or cut some fat from the steak and rub around in the pan. Do not use butter as it will not get hot enough without burning. Let it get good 'n hot.

Lay the steak in the hot pan and sear it on both sides to hold as much juice as possible. Then fry until done to your liking. Place on a towel for just a moment on both sides to absorb any grease. Rub both sides with melted butter. Quickly place steak on a warm plate and serve.

As with any cookware, Dutch ovens came in a variety of sizes to meet the needs of a wide consumer base. On a trail drive, however, the cookie normally carried one pot that could accommodate the largest number of eaters he thought he would feed. This eliminated the transport of unwanted items and freed valuable chuck wagon space for other more important supplies such as flour, rice, salt pork, bacon, and other essentials.

Helava Chili

- 2–3 pounds of chopped beef
- 4 tablespoons bacon drippings
- 1 large diced onion
- Green chilies to taste
- 1 eight-ounce can of tomatoes
- 4 tablespoons chili powder
- 2 tablespoons cumin
- 4 cloves garlic
- ½ teaspoon oregano
- 1 cup water
- Pinch of cayenne
- Salt and pepper to taste
- Pinch of thyme

In a Dutch oven, brown the beef in the bacon fat (do not drain). Add the onions and green chilies, and continue to cook for a few more minutes. Add remaining ingredients; simmer for at least an hour, stirring occasionally. Do not cover unless you're cooking outdoors. Add a little more water whenever it looks like it is going to stick. Skim the grease when well cooked. Thicken with 2 tablespoons flour mixed with ¼ cup water. Stir and cook another 10–20 minutes.

Serve the chili over beans, refried beans, rice, biscuits, or cornbread. You can add beans to the chili but most cowboy cooks made it separate; it offered more options.

Chuck Wagon Scrapple

Scrapple is made of cornmeal mush and meat scraps—traditionally from a hog's head. This recipe is a little more universal.

- 2 pounds pork sausage
- 2 ½ quarts of water
- Three finger pinch the following: sage, poultry seasoning, parsley, and salt
- 4 cups cornmeal

Brown the sausage in a Dutch oven. Add water and bring to a boil. Add all seasonings and stir well. Mix the cornmeal with 2 cups cold water. Slowly stir cornmeal mixture into dutch oven and cook for 2–3 minutes. Spoon into loaf pans and chill. When well chilled, invert the pan and remove the scrapple by gently shaking it. Slice and fry in grease until crispy. Serve warm with syrup.

DUTCH OVEN COOKING INSTRUCTIONS

The way to savor the flavors and aromas of the old west is to cook outside over open flames in a Dutch oven. Dutch ovens have always been an important item for the westward traveler. Lewis and Clark and the Corps of Discovery carried a ready supply of cast-iron Dutch oven cookware to meet their needs. Pioneers heading to the gold fields of California and homesteaders looking to till the virgin prairie soil all took with them their old reliable cookware.

Splatterdabs

The name "Splatterdabs" carries a different connotation depending on whom you speak with. These are different from regular hotcakes because they do not use eggs and in some cases could be made without milk as well, making them easy to cook on the trail.

- 1 quart flour
- 2 tablespoons baking powder
- 2 teaspoons sugar
- 1 teaspoon salt
- Bacon grease
- Milk or water

Mix all dry ingredients together. Then add milk or water to make a thick but pourable batter. Pour into heated skillet that has been liberally greased. As edges appear to get stiff, flip and cook the other side until done. Serve with syrup and butter if available.

Splatterdabs, hot cakes, griddle cakes—no matter what the name they were an easy staple to fill the growling stomach on the trail and in the prairie home. Mattie Oblinger, a prairie housewife, wrote a letter to family and friends lauding her new recipe for pancakes that did not require milk or eggs. If syrup was not available, fresh fruit, butter, cinnamon, sugar, jam, and marmalade were also used to sweeten the hot, fluffy cakes. If splatterdabs were overcooked, cowboys might relegate them to target practice or horseshoe substitutes.

Corn Fritters

For this recipe, fresh corn removed from the cobs works the best.

- 1 ¼ cups flour
- 2 cups fresh corn
- 1 teaspoon baking powder
- 2 teaspoons salt
- ½ cup sugar
- ¼ teaspoon paprika
- 2 eggs
- ¼ cup milk

Stir dry ingredients together and add the corn. Then add the egg yolks beaten thick. Fold in egg whites beaten stiff. Fry in hot lard or other oil. Remove from oil and daub off any excess grease and serve hot.

Rice and Onions

- 1 quart of prepared rice
- 1 small diced onion
- 2 tablespoons salt pork drippings
- Salt and pepper

In a heavy pot, over medium-high heat, melt drippings until very hot. Add onion pieces and fry until they begin to clear. Add rice and stir while it continues to fry. Fry for just a few minutes and serve hot.

The above recipe offers good flavor and is an example of how rice was used by the wagon cook. This provided variety in the menu on the trail. Often beans of various kinds and other vegetables that offered flavor were added to rice. Rice was, like sugar, flour, sourdough, dried beans, and spices, easy to transport in the chuck wagon and survived the rigors of the trail.

Cowboy Beans

- 2 cups dried red beans
- 2 cups dried pinto beans
- 1 large yellow onion, chopped
- 3 tablespoons garlic, chopped
- 3 green chili peppers, grilled and diced
- 3 vine-ripened tomatoes, grilled, seeded, and chopped
- 1 tablespoon lard
- 7 quarts water
- 1 smoked ham hock
- 1 teaspoon toasted coriander seed
- 1 bay leaf
- 2 whole dried red chili peppers
- Salt and pepper, to taste

Serves 16 hungry cowboys on the trail

Soak beans overnight in water to cover, changing water once, then draining. When beans are ready, sauté onion, garlic, green chilies, and tomatoes in lard in a large Dutch oven over medium-high heat. Add water and ham hock and bring to a boil. Then add beans, coriander seed, bay leaf, and dried chilies. Continue boiling for 30 minutes or so, then lower heat, cover, and simmer for several hours (3 to 4) or until beans are tender.

Chuck Wagon Stew

- 2 ½ pounds beef, cut into cubes
- 2 tablespoons flour
- 1 tablespoon paprika
- 1 teaspoon chili powder, for coating
- 2 teaspoons salt
- 3 tablespoons lard
- 2 large onions, sliced
- 1 clove of garlic, minced well
- Several large tomatoes
- 3 tablespoons chili powder, more if you want
- 1 tablespoon cinnamon
- 1 teaspoon ground cloves
- 2 cups chopped potatoes
- 2 cups chopped carrots

Coat the beef cubes in a mixture of flour, paprika, chili powder, and salt.

Brown in hot fat in a large Dutch oven. Add onions and garlic and cook until soft; add tomatoes, chili powder, cinnamon, and cloves. Cover and simmer for 2 hours and then add potatoes and carrots and cook until vegetables are done, about 45 minutes to 1 hour, or as needed.

Stew that was prepared while on the trail would use whatever game was available: buffalo, elk, venison, or prairie chicken. The cowboys might bring beef among their rations, but animals from the herd were only slaughtered on the trail if needed, generally due to illness or injury.

Today, historians, cowboy poets and singers, and chuck wagon cooks and racers keep the spirit of the Old West alive. Each year chuck wagons take to the trails to teach a new generation of youngsters enamored with the cowboy way of life about the importance of that time in our nation's past. Chuck wagon cooking competitions, chuck wagon races, and cowboy action shooting organizations all provide a glimpse into the life of the American West minus the dust, danger, and hardships that our pioneering ancestors endured so long ago. Spending a day with a cookie gives you a greater appreciation for those hearty men who drove the wagons that fed hungry cowboys on the trail. Josh Hoy, of the Flying W Ranch near Cedar Point, Kansas, shares some of his favorite recipes and the memories of growing up in Flint Hills ranch country.

Bacon and Beans

- 1 slab of bacon
- ⅓ cup of beans per person, rinsed and soaked
- Onions, chopped
- Chili peppers
- Salt

Cut bacon into as many pieces as there are men to feed. Fry the bacon, onions, and chilies in the bean pot, then add beans. Add enough water to just cover the beans. Simmer until tender. Don't salt until 5 minutes before serving.

Chili Beef

- ½ pound of beef per man
- Onions
- Chili peppers
- Wine or vinegar
- 1 quart canned tomatoes
- Molasses
- Salt

Cut beef into as many pieces as there are men to feed; 1 joint bone, a section of ox tail, several ribs, or a broken marrow bone—any of these will work.

Brown beef chunks and bones in Dutch oven or covered kettle. Add onions and chilies and brown. Add wine or vinegar, tomatoes, molasses, and salt to taste. Simmer while covered for 3 or 4 hours.

Sourdough Starter

- Flour
- Water
- Sugar

In an uncovered crock pot, mix 2 cups flour, 2 cups water, and 1 tablespoon sugar. Cover with a dirty dish rag. Let stand in a warm spot 4 days before using. Add water and flour as used. You can keep this starter going for generations.

Sourdough Biscuits

- 3 or 4 cups of flour
- Butter
- 1 cup starter
- 1 teaspoon salt
- 1 tablespoon sugar
- ½ cup lard
- Suet (or any rendered fat)

Cut butter or other fat into flour. Make a well of the flour and mix in remaining ingredients until just stiff. Grease your hands and pinch the dough into a Dutch oven. Bake about 15 minutes.

Bake carefully. No jury will convict a cowboy of assault if the biscuits are burned or of battery if they are soggy.

Trammel Rushing of the Rushing Wagon of El Reno, Oklahoma, has the distinction of being a nationally recognized chuck wagon cook. In addition to having an original Army freight wagon that was converted into a chuck wagon, Trammel is also a great storyteller and has a wealth of information about chuck wagon life. Here, Trammel shares some the Rushing Wagon's favorite recipes that you can easily make today.

Confederate Coffee Cake
—THE WALKING T RANCH

- 1 cup sugar
- ½ cup butter
- ½ cup milk
- 3 eggs
- 1 ½ cups flour
- 2 teaspoons baking powder
- Nutmeg, cinnamon, chopped nut meats (almonds, walnuts, or pecans)

Cream sugar and butter, add milk and eggs, and mix well. Sift the flour and baking powder, blend with the sugar and butter, and add a dash of nutmeg. Pour into a well-greased pan and sprinkle the top with nutmeg, cinnamon, nuts, and granulated sugar. Dot the top with butter.

Bake at 350 degrees for 30 minutes or until a toothpick inserted in the center comes out clean.

Beef Tips

—Lytle Bend Ranch

- 2 pounds rib-eye, cut into chunks (any cut of meat can be substituted)
- 1 onion, chopped
- 1 tablespoon bacon grease or oil
- 2 quarts water
- Salt and pepper

Generously salt and pepper beef and brown with onions in oil. Add water. Simmer for 1 hour until tender.

Smothered Steak

—XX-Ranch

- ¼ cup flour
- ½ teaspoon salt
- ½ teaspoon pepper
- Grease or shortening
- 1 small onion, chopped
- ½ green pepper
- 1 stalk celery, diced
- 1 small can tomatoes

Beat flour, salt, and pepper into meat. Brown meat in shortening; add the remaining ingredients and cook for 1½ hours.

Beef Tenders

—KING RANCH

- 1 pound beef tenders (tenderloin); may substitute 1 pound cubed sirloin
- 1 pinch garlic
- ¼ cup flour
- Salt and pepper to taste
- Plain rice, cooked

Gravy
- 1 tablespoon flour
- Water

Mix garlic and flour, season meat with garlic and flour mixture. Brown tenders in a heavy frying pan, simmer for 5 minutes. Serve with rice and gravy.

To Make Gravy: Add 1 cup water to pan juices. Mix 1 tablespoon flour in ¼ cup water, stir into hot pan juices a little at a time.

Texas Beef Tips

—WAGON CREEK RANCH

- 2 pounds sirloin cut into 1-inch cubes
- 1 tablespoon grease (use more if necessary)
- 1 clove garlic, slashed
- ½ package Lipton onion soup mix
- 1 tablespoon Tabasco Sauce
- 1 tablespoon A-1 Steak Sauce
- 1–2 cups water
- 1 medium onion, chopped
- 1 jalapeno pepper, chopped
- 2 tablespoons corn starch

Use a 14-inch Dutch oven for this recipe. Brown meat in grease. Add garlic and soup mix and stir until soup mix dissolves. Add Tabasco sauce, A-1 sauce, and water. Cook until all blends in, about 3 minutes. Add jalapeno and corn starch. Mix all together and simmer on low heat for 2 hours.

Roast Beef

- 2 ½ pounds roast beef
- 4 tablespoons lemon pepper
- 4–5 tablespoons garlic powder
- 2 teaspoons paprika
- 2 teaspoons oregano
- 2 teaspoons marjoram
- Salt to taste
- 4 tablespoons black pepper

Serves 5

Season roast with seasonings. Let stand for 2 hours. Cook in Dutch oven slowly for 3 hours.

Cowpoke Beans

—6666 RANCH

"You've got to treat these little pinto beans the same way you would a new born colt—with a lot of love and attention."—Richard Bolt, 6666 Ranch

- 1 pound dried pinto beans
- 2 ½ cups cold water
- ½ pound salt pork, cut up
- 1 red chili pepper
- 1 medium onion, chopped
- 1 clove garlic, minced
- 1 six-ounce can tomato paste
- 1 ½ tablespoons chili powder
- 1 tablespoon salt
- 1 teaspoon cumin seed
- ½ teaspoon marjoram

Serves 8

Wash and pick over beans and put in a mixing bowl. Cover beans with cold water and soak overnight. The next morning put the beans and cold water in a Dutch oven, and bring it to a boil. Reduce heat, cover, and simmer for 1 hour. Stir in remaining ingredients and simmer 3 hours or until tender. Add water if necessary.

Ketcham Canyon Stew

—IXL RANCH

- 8 strips thick sliced bacon, chopped
- ⅓ cup unbleached flour
- Salt and ½ teaspoon ground black pepper
- 1 teaspoon thyme or dried sage
- 2 ½ pounds beef chuck or bottom round cut into 1 ½-inch cubes
- ¾ cup chopped onion
- 1 ½ cups strong coffee
- 3 tablespoons chili sauce or ketchup
- 2 tablespoons molasses
- 2 tablespoons Worchester sauce
- 18 small boiling onions, peeled
- 6 small red potatoes, peeled and quartered
- 4 carrots, peeled and cut in 1 ½-inch lengths
- Chopped fresh parsley

In a Dutch oven over medium heat, cook bacon slowly to render the fat. Remove the cooked bacon with a slotted spoon and set aside. Combine flour, 1 teaspoon salt, pepper, and thyme or sage. Pat the beef cubes dry and toss with flour mixture. Over medium-high heat, brown the beef in bacon drippings, working in batches, if necessary. Remove the browned meat and set aside. Add the chopped onion to the pan and cook 1–2 minutes. Stir in coffee, chili sauce, molasses, Worchester sauce, reserved beef, and bacon. Cover and simmer over low heat for 1 hour stirring occasionally.

Add the onions and 3 cups of water. Simmer covered for 30 minutes. Stir in potatoes, carrots and more water if necessary. Continue to simmer the stew partially covered for about 30 minutes or until the potatoes and carrots are tender. Add salt to taste and serve garnished with fresh parsley.

Sage Biscuits

- 2 cups all purpose flour
- 4 teaspoons baking powder
- 1 teaspoon salt
- 1 teaspoon rubbed dried sage
- ½ teaspoon cumin seed
- 6 tablespoons shortening
- ¾ cup milk
- 2 teaspoons light corn syrup
- 1 teaspoon water

Combine flour, baking powder, salt, sage, and cumin in mixing bowl. Cut in shortening until crumbly. Add milk and mix to moisten flour. Shape into a ball, turn out on a lightly floured surface. Roll or pat into an 8-inch circle, cut into 6 wedges (it may be cut with floured 2½-inch round cutter). Brush tops with mixture of corn syrup and water. Bake on ungreased dish or sheet at 450 degrees for about 12 minutes until brown.

Trammel Rushing and his wife Susan won first in cooking, first in wagon, and the all-around in food and wagon awards with this recipe at the Pawnee Bill Ranch in Pawnee, Oklahoma, in 1998. This was their very first chuck wagon cooking competition.

Eating a bowl of chili, grilling a superb steak, or cooking up a mess of pancakes all are part of the legacy of the American West and the life of the cowboy on the trail.

Why I'm a Grass-Fed Beef Rancher

America's cattle have been fed grain for so long generations of people believe that's how they evolved. Marbled, corn-fed steaks have been marketed into our consciousness as the best we could eat.

Then I learned that Mother Nature didn't plan it that way. Grass is their natural diet. Corn makes them fatter faster. The fat makes them tasty. The price we pay is in nutrition.

It seemed like a good time to return the modern bovine to its rightful home—the pasture. No one was brave enough to tell me it wasn't going to be easy. Many ranchers had tried to go back to the old ways of finishing their cattle on grass, but they failed because the meat was tough, or they couldn't fatten the animals when winter turned the grass brown, or they couldn't find a market. Ranchers raise cattle; as a rule, they're not salesmen, promoters, or advertising executives.

The grassy road to success was littered with broken cowboy dreams. Still, as the sun came up over the big blue stem east of my ranch house a year ago, I felt the entrepreneur's ghostly spirit set my skin to tingling. And I knew instinctively—times had changed.

The first sign was Dr. Allen Williams and his partner Dr. Matt Cravey. Like the explorers Stanley and Livingstone, they had found each other during a mutual quest to locate the perfect grass-fed animal, one with genes that made it tender, tasty, and able to fatten quickly on nothing but grass, just the way those first English breeds from the Mayflower did. Most of those original genetic profiles had been scrambled out of existence when the corn tsunami swept away those lovely, salad-bar days in the pasture sixty years ago. But Williams and Cravey were relentless, searching herd after herd for beef's holy grail.

Lesser men would have folded, discouraged by too many bad rib-eyes in the small, dusty watering holes of Montana. But not this duo. They were following a vision, dreaming that a few of those genetically perfect grass-feeders had survived and were actually grazing on little islands of forage dotting the American pasture where they had been stranded by the giant wave of corn. But how would they know? There was no bovine DNA databank to find a match. Still, modern science would provide the eureka moment.

Backing his pick-up into the corral, Dr. Williams lowers the tailgate and pulls out an ordinary looking computer attached to a long cable that connects to a . . . wand. Yes, an ultrasound machine. That in itself is nothing to raise an eyebrow. It's what comes on the screen that drops the jaw of any leather-faced old-timer in the yard. There, in its digital-age glory, is a picture of a rib-eye muscle on a living

animal. Filtered through the carefully programmed brain of Drs. Williams and Cravey, the process produces a consistent judgment of tenderness. Like Alexander slicing through the Gordian knot, it cut the primary obstacle standing in the way of the grass-fed beef revolution—how to consistently deliver quality.

With the right genetic heritage it was clear that pure grass-fed and grass-finished cattle could be as tender as the best prime beef. It was enough to

begin planning a start-up, the Tallgrass Beef Company. To our surprise, everyone we talked with said, *"What took you so long?"*

But there was another unknown that had to be answered before full launch: the matter of taste. We gathered some potential investors at one of Chicago's premier steak houses, Harry Caray's. Out came a tray of tasting samples: filet, rib-eye, hamburger, and New York strip, carefully cut into small portions so that the eight people sitting around the table could taste each piece of meat. Just like a Napa Valley wine tasting.

The hush was agonizing. They chewed slowly as if savoring the body of a smooth burgundy. Then, from the other side of the table came a comment. "I've traded cattle on the Mercantile for forty years and this is the best steak I've ever tasted." Everyone concurred. And everyone invested based on tenderness and taste as pure as the prairie.

We decided then and there that we didn't have to make any apologies because our meat was "grass-fed." We now put it up against prime as an alternative on the beef menu offering the original taste of deep beef flavor, a steak that you want to spend time with. To be truly grass-fed and grass-finished, we

knew we'd have to be all-natural. Eliminating artificial hormones and antibiotics to create a healthier product was not a hard decision. From all the uproar about them—even a ban by Europe on our hormone-injected meat—their banishment seemed inevitable anyway.

Although we knew that a rising tide of consumers were searching for natural items, we were surprised at how many consumers were already choosing products with labels promoting omega-3 fatty acids and CLAs, something unheard of just a few years earlier. Silently, they were seeking out healthy alternatives and driving a brand new trend. Organic

sections in supermarkets were increasing at a rate of 20 percent a year. The Baby Boomers had entered the food revolution. Our timing was perfect . . . accidentally. But there's more.

In addition to catching the wave of the natural food movement, I was making other discoveries about grass-fed beef. Grass-fed and -finished beef transforms the much-maligned red meat that doctors take off their heart patient's plates into a health food. I put on my reporter's old green eye shade and plunged into the worlds of medical research and molecular biology with a properly skeptical eye.

The first thing I learned is that essential fatty acids (EFAs) have become the darling of the health food business. Paul Stitt, a biochemist, told a Canadian conference in 1988 that two hundred studies are published per month on fatty acids, and to date more than 350,000 have been catalogued on lipids and fats. Two fatty acids in particular have become celebrities, omega-3 and omega-6. They function down at the cellular level to regulate what goes in and what is kept out of cells. They help keep cell membranes fluid and flexible. Without the proper balance of these two fatty acids, cells can become stiff, unhealthy, and full of problems. Since so many diseases, like cancer, start at the cellular level, researchers have targeted EFAs for extensive study.

Omega-3 fatty acids are found primarily in green leafy vegetables, flax, and oils extracted from cold-water fish like mackerel, salmon, tuna, or cod. It is also found in animals that graze in green pastures, just like the wild game early man ate millions of years ago. Iceland is currently marketing its population's longevity as the oldest in the world, thanks to a diet rich in omega-3 that comes from cold water fish caught off its shore. Like the Tin Man in *The Wizard of Oz* who locked up from a lack of oil, the omega-3 fatty acids keep the fish from stiffening up in the frigid waters. And they do the same for our cells. And you may have heard about the headline-making 2002 study in the *Journal of the American Medical Association* which concluded that eating fish (with omega-3s) once per month or more can reduce the risk of ischemic stroke in men. One final example: Dr. Barry Sears, who wrote *The Zone*, believes *Homo sapiens* avoided extinction and became a more cognitive being, able to conquer the world, by finding a food source high in omega-3s: shellfish along the shores of Lake Turkana in the East African Rift Valley. The shellfish ate algae and accumulated algae-derived fats in higher concentrations that were, in turn, full of omega-3s. These fats supplied the brain with blood glucose, and they laid the foundation for a new species: modern humans.

Today, everyone agrees that these fatty acids are labeled "essential" for a reason. They are absolutely necessary for a body to function properly. They concur on something else. We can't create EFAs inside our bodies, on our own. The only way we can get them is from what we eat. Water and air are good examples. If we don't get enough of those "essentials," we know what happens pretty fast. Researchers are suspicious of what is happening to us by not getting enough fatty acids because over the last hundred years, EFAs, like omega-3s, have disappeared from the typical American diet. If these essential fatty acids (EFAs) are absolutely necessary, and if they are no longer found in our diet or are far out of balance, then aren't we killing ourselves? Let's face it: our diet has changed. Industrialized mass food production, ocean pollution, and refining of supermarket food have caused a severe deficiency in omega-3 fatty acids in our diet while increasing the fatty acid omega-6, Darth Vader among the EFAs. Human beings evolved with omega-6 and omega-3 in a 1:1 ratio, eating a diet of nuts, plants, and wild game. The modern ratio can often be 10:1, even 20:1 omega-6 to omega-3. That's a bad balance, considering that omega-6 can cause tumors, chronic inflammation, heart disease, stroke, diabetes, arthritis, and auto-immunity when not held in check by the omega-3 fatty acid.

A good case study is the American beef industry. Corn is as unnatural for cattle as fast food is for humans. Cows are ruminants that have evolved multi-chambered stomachs to break down cellulose from grass, not corn. Grain-based feeds create different bacteria within the cow's rumen. It's unnatural. We can't put just anything we want into our mouths, or into those of the animals we eat, and expect them to magically change it into something healthy? The out-of-balance ratio—omega-6s to omega-3s—changes back to normal when the cattle eat grass.

An Irish study published in the *Journal of Animal Science* in 2000 proved that when steers are fed grass, they have a lower omega-6 to omega-3 ratio than steers fed concentrates. The Irish grass-fed animals also showed a higher concentration of conjugated linoleic acid, or CLA, than grain-fed steers. CLA? Don't tell me it's another miracle ingredient. Although it's still at an early stage of research, there are indications that it may have remarkable curative properties. Chemist Darshan S. Kelley, at the University of California, Davis says of CLA, "It has stimulated animals' immune systems, reduced body fat, protected against certain kinds of cancer, and improved cardiovascular health." To be fair, he also says that those were animal studies and recommends that human studies should proceed before conclusions are drawn.

Regardless of the balance of omegas, big, juicy, corn-fed prime steaks won't go out of style. The grain-fed model has been all America could get for the last sixty years, and steak lovers have developed a taste for it. But as boomers swell into the meat sections of supermarkets, as young mothers read the labels before they serve their children, and as young people, armed with the knowledge coming from the wealth of new nutritional discoveries, search for a change in the food they eat, they will find grass-fed and -finished beef.

In creating the Tallgrass Beef Company we felt our consumers should know what we are trying to do and what we stand for. We let our cattle do the talking:

- I am Tallgrass Beef.
- I am the future of America's beef.
- I am a pure, natural product of the Great American Prairie; the best, healthiest, and most delicious brand of grass-fed and -raised beef you can buy.
- I come from rare genetic stock whose historic origins are verified and fully traceable, ensuring that you always enjoy delicious, healthy beef.
- I come from cattle that spent their lives on open range or improved pastures eating only natural forages. No synthetic growth hormones, animal by-products, or antibiotics were ever involved in my production.
- I come from cattle that were never forced to eat grain, nor spend any part of their life in a feedlot.
- I come from ranchers and farmers who treat all their animals in a humane manner from birth to harvest.
- I come from good stewards of the land—independent ranchers and farmers who raise cattle in a time-honored manner that sustains and enriches the environment.
- I taste as good as the best prime beef, but I am better for your health.
- I am Tallgrass Beef.

As for me, that's why I'm a grass-fed rancher.
Bill Kurtis

chapter 5

The Modern Prairie Table

> [The Kansas prairie] is not the gorgeous woman you dreamed should someday be yours, but she is mystery and tenderness and strength and rapture, and suddenly you know that this is what you wanted all your life.
>
> —Zula Bennington Greene

Recipes from Famous Cowboys and Great Chefs

For the family that sits at the modern prairie table it is difficult to escape the past. The past lives and breathes in the blades of slender, graceful grass that tower skyward reaching for the sun. The past lives in the land and way of life that is passed from generation to generation. Every bowl of stew, every pot of chili, each succulent steak spiced and grilled to perfection, every morsel of cornbread, and each drop of good strong coffee speaks of the prairie past that we have explored together. No industry pays greater homage to the past than agriculture in the cattle ranching and grazing areas of the American West.

The recipes in this chapter come from the cutting-edge kitchens of modern chefs, and the kitchens of modern prairie cooks and celebrity cowboys of the past, all of whom have made the West a part of the American identity. There's even a great recipe from the Mayor of Dodge City, Kansas, one of the original cattle towns.

Judy Tolbert of Sedan, Kansas, a true modern prairie cook, honors her family's history with each dish that is created in her kitchen. Dedicating her energies to promoting small town life in Sedan, Kansas—home of Bill Kurtis's Red Buffalo Ranch—Judy learned her love of cooking from her grandmother who was a Kansas pioneer in her own right.

Broccoli-Cauliflower Salad

—JUDY TOLBERT

- 1 head broccoli
- 1 head cauliflower
- 8-10 green onions, diced
- 1 pound bacon, diced and fried crisp
- 1 cup dried cranberries
- ¼ cup spanish olives, cut in half
- ¼ cup chopped walnuts
- 1 cup mayonnaise
- ⅓ cup sugar (can use Splenda for diabetics)
- 1 teaspoon garlic salt
- 2 teaspoons vinegar
- 1 cup shredded colby jack cheese

Cut broccoli and cauliflower into bite size pieces. Mix with onions, bacon, cranberries, olives, and walnuts.

Combine sugar, garlic salt, vinegar, and mayonnaise. Pour evenly over the above ingredients. Do not stir.

Sprinkle cheese on top. Refrigerate overnight.

Beef Roll-Ups
with Whiskey Butter Sauce

—JUDY TOLBERT

- Tallgrass beef flank steak (approx. 2 pounds) pounded to approx. ¼-inch thin, cut into strips
- 3–4 tablespoons minced garlic
- 3 tablespoons minced fresh parsley
- 2 large eggs plus 2 tablespoons water to make an egg wash
- 2 cups bread crumbs (finely processed)
- ½ pound deli-sliced Harvati cheese

Whiskey Butter Sauce
- 2 teaspoons minced garlic
- 2 teaspoons finely chopped shallots
- 2 cups whiskey
- 1 ½ cups cold butter cut into pieces

On each steak strip place a small strip of cheese, top with garlic and parsley, roll up, and secure with toothpicks. Dip in egg wash and roll in bread crumbs to coat. Deep fry in peanut oil at 350 degrees until golden brown, about 6 minutes. I keep them hot on a baking sheet lined with parchment paper in the oven while the rest are cooking.

Serve with Whiskey Butter Sauce topped with sprigs of fresh parsley to garnish.

In a large skillet, add garlic, shallots, and whiskey. Carefully place over the flame and cook until reduced by half. Allow the flames to die down. Remove from fire and begin whisking in the butter. Return to heat occasionally to heat the mixture slightly, continuing until all the butter is added and the mixture is smooth.

No prairie supper is complete without fresh bread. Judy adds, "In the summer, I grow my own herbs and make fresh herb bread. I process leftover bread in my food processor so that I have seasoned bread crumbs on hand. I serve this bread with a mixture of white truffle oil and balsamic vinegar."

Sometimes quick cooking is the order of the day. For the chuck wagon and prairie cooks of the nineteenth century the microwave and other time-saving inventions were not an option and cooking was at times a tedious, time-consuming affair. Steve Katz is a food writer and author who attributes his cooking skills and knowledge—particularly regarding beef—to growing up in Chicago where his family owned Stock Yards Packing Company, a premier purveyor of prime beef to hotels and restaurants.

His earliest memories include the International Livestock Exposition in Chicago in 1960 where his father and uncles bought the Grand Champion Steer—a Hereford named Herky—partnering with a restaurant in Las Vegas that rolled out wheel barrows full of silver dollars in payment. Fittingly, Steve Katz received a ribbon for Cowboy Steaks in a Skillet at a cattleman's convention with "Cowboy Poet" Baxter Black on hand to perform!

Cowboy Steaks in a Skillet

—STEVE KATZ

- 2 butterflied twelve-ounce (or 4 six-ounce) Tallgrass Beef New York Strip steaks
- 1 large Spanish onion, sliced into medium thick rings
- 1 large green pepper, long slices about ½-inch wide
- 3 tablespoons olive oil
- 1 tablespoon butter or margarine
- 1 teaspoon paprika or southwestern red roasted chili powder (not hot)
- 1 tablespoon chopped fresh cilantro or parsley
- 1 teaspoon Kosher salt

Serves 2 hungry cowboys or 4 townsfolk

Season beef as desired with seasoning salt or celery salt; trim fat from side of steaks before butterflying.

Place 12-inch (or larger) cast iron skillet on low to medium heat. Melt butter in pan, then add olive oil and salt. Add onions to pan. Coat with oil, butter, and salt. Add paprika or other ground roasted red pepper and mix with onions. Add cilantro or parsley and mix well. Turn heat to medium-high. Add 1 tablespoon water, cover pan, and cook for 5 minutes.

(recipe continues on next page)

Cowboy Steaks in a Skillet (continued)

Remove cover and mix onions with spatula, continuing to cook until translucent and golden. Push onions to side of pan. Add green peppers and brown. Mix onions and green peppers together and move to side of pan. Turning heat up to high, place steaks into pan and sear each side quickly for about 1 minute on each side to brown. Use tongs to check. Remove pan from heat, place onions and pepper on top of the steaks, and cover pan. Let sit on cool burner stovetop for 10 minutes for medium, longer for well. Steaks will be ready and a rich sauce will be waiting in the pan!

Serve steaks on oval platter with bed of onions and green pepper and sauce spooned over steaks. Serve with Texas toast triangles for mopping up the sauce.

The cowboy on the silver screen has done more to make the cowboy a true American icon than the original cowboys themselves. For many young boys their first introduction to the cowboy was in a musty theatre on Saturday morning. Later generations would learn of the travails of trail life from television programs like *The Chuck Wagon*, *Bonanza*, *The Big Valley*, and of course *Gunsmoke*. What did many of the world's most recognizable celluloid cowboys eat? Here are some celebrity cowboy and cowgirl favorites.

Will Rogers's Favorite Chili

"I SURE DO LOVE MY CHILI."—WILL ROGERS, JULY 17, 1927

After consulting family members and scrapbooks, the children of Will Rogers discovered their father's favorite dish. " . . . I have checked with mother's sisters and my own sister and brother, and we all agree that dad's favorite dish was beans. Any style, any kind . . . Mother's sister, Aunt Theda, recalls a recipe that dad particularly liked, and after digging into her scrapbook, found the following."

- 1 pound ground round steak
- 1 onion, chopped
- Salt to taste
- 1 can tomatoes
- 1 can (small) pimento, chopped
- 2 cans red kidney beans

Sauté meat in skillet with onions and salt until slightly brown. Add tomatoes and pimento. Place in hot oven for about 1 hour, then add red kidney beans, stir and continue cooking for 30 to 45 minutes.

Homemade Meatloaf

—GENE AUTRY

"Gene loved this meatloaf and often requested it. I made it for him more times than I can count. Hope you enjoy it."—Jackie Autry

- 1 ½ pounds ground beef
- 1 medium onion, chopped
- 1 cup fresh tomatoes, chopped
- 1 cup ketchup
- 2 eggs
- 1 ¼ cup oatmeal
- Salt and pepper to taste

Serves 8

Preheat oven to 350 degrees. Combine all ingredients. Pack lightly into a loaf and bake for about 1 ½ hours.

Quick Chili-Tex

—DALE EVANS

Even the busiest cowgirl likes a good western-inspired meal! For today's modern cowgirls time is of the essence when cooking.

- 1 large can chili with beans
- Grated cheese
- 1 medium can yellow or white hominy
- Chopped onions

Serves 4–6

Heat oven to 350 degrees. Alternate layers of chili with beans, cheese, and hominy in baking dish. Top with more grated cheese and bake until onions are tender and cheese is melted.

Large wide-brimmed hat, ornate chaps, the best boots money can buy, and round wire-rimmed bookish glasses hardly paint a portrait of a trail-hardened cowboy. While most Americans are familiar with the famous Phillips 66 signs that dotted American highways and byways, they are not as familiar with the enigmatic founder of Phillips Petroleum, Frank Phillips. A devotee of the American West and all that goes with it, Frank was not only an avid fan of the cowboy but of the American Indian as well. He holds the honor of being made an honorary chief of the Osage in the Bartlesville, Oklahoma area. His ranch and game preserve, Woolaroc, was the backdrop for the annual Cow Thieves and Outlaws gatherings, where the cowboy life was extolled. Here we replicate Frank's recipe for Pheasant à la King with a few minor variations.

Pheasant à la King (Revised 3/11/1948)

—FRANK PHILLIPS

- 1 cup pheasant meat (prepared as directed)
- Salt
- 8–9 tablespoons melted butter
- ½ cup heavy or light cream
- ½ cup milk
- 1 tablespoon flour
- 1 green pepper
- ½ can pimento, cut into small pieces
- 1 small can fancy mushroom buttons

Roasting

First, cut the bird into 2 pieces, 1 piece comprised of the legs and the other piece the breast, back, and neck. Then split the leg saddle into 2 pieces. Next, cut the neck, with backbone attached, from the breast. The use of a pair of heavy shears or tin-snips will facilitate in cutting up the bird. This operation will give 4 pieces: the 2 legs with thighs attached, the breast, and the neck with the backbone attached.

(recipe continues on next page)

Pheasant à la King
(continued)

A pheasant can be best cleaned by washing (if it is not washed and plucked already). Do not hesitate to skin the bird (if it is not already). You may have been told that removal of the skin from the pheasant causes it to dry out during cooking and will cause a loss of flavor. Forget it—the taste of this dish will not be impaired by skinning the pheasant.

Place the pieces of the bird in a Pyrex dish or roaster, uncovered, then sprinkle with salt, using 1 teaspoonful for each piece. Then cover the pieces of bird with a piece of cloth just large enough to cover them. Pour melted butter (2 tablespoons per piece) over the cloth. Place the vessel containing the bird in an oven at 250 degrees. Be sure to check oven temperature. After 1 hour baste every 30 minutes. Roast for 4½ hours and then remove dish from the oven. Save the small amount of liquid resulting from the cooking of the pheasant, permitting it to remain in the dish. Allow to cool and remove the meat from the bones of the pheasant, carefully removing the small pieces of broken bone caused by birdshot.

(recipe continues on next page)

Pheasant à la King
(continued)

Preparation

Try to follow the proportions of the ingredients as shown below. These proportions are for 1 cup of pheasant meat.

Cut pheasant meat into fairly large pieces. Do not cut the meat too finely. ½-inch by 1-inch is about right. Combine 2 parts milk and 1 part heavy cream to make 1 cup of liquid. If light cream is available use more of it and you will obtain approximately the same amount of cream in the total mixture. Add 1 tablespoon (level) of flour to milk and cream mixture, shake vigorously in a fruit jar or stir in order to thoroughly dissolve the flour. Add ½ teaspoonful of salt to the entire cream–flour mixture and shake well. Remove green pepper heads and cut pepper into small pieces. After thoroughly draining the diced peppers, place them in a skillet or Pyrex dish and add butter. Then heat and stir over a very low flame until the peppers show a decided change in color. This will require about 20 minutes. Next add the mushrooms to the peppers and continue stirring and heating over the low flame for about 5 minutes. Then add the peppers and mushrooms to the vessel with the pheasant meat, mixing the ingredients thoroughly and place in the oven at 250 degrees for about 30 minutes to have the mixture hot before adding the remaining ingredients.

Pour the milk–cream–flour mixture as prepared above in an open pyrex baking dish or skillet and heat over a very low flame until the mixture starts to boil gently, stirring continuously to prevent scorching. Continue gentle boiling for about 3 minutes. Now add this hot cream sauce to the hot mixture of the pheasant meat, peppers, and mushrooms and then add the remaining ingredient (pimento) and thoroughly mix. Serve hot, preferably over dry toast or wild rice.

Baxter Black needs no introduction to devotees of the cowboy lifestyle. Poet, humorist, and large-animal veterinarian, Baxter's contributions to National Public Radio have brought the wit and wisdom of the West to countless Americans in cities and small towns alike. Baxter shares his recipe for beans as only he can!

Beans à la Black
A recipe for trouble

—BAXTER BLACK

Down through the ages, the humble bean has been treated as the blue collar worker of the menu. The landscape on the plate, the flannel sheets for the plump weenie to lay its head. Always there, usually unnoticed like rice in China, cows in Westerns, and duplicity in Congress. It has assumed the supporting role, never asking to carry the ball, ride Trigger, get the girl, or have a speaking part. Deferring always to the filet, fajita, or French onion soup. And, even though it is a famous food in its own right, it is frijoles fame . . . like owning the most expensive Ford Escort.

Thus, to rectify this culinary snobbery I offer my recipe for Beans à la Black.

- ½ pound dried pinto beans
- Capers, raspberries, pearl onions (several of each)
- Chili powder
- Lime juice

Select 22 blemish-free beans. Boil till soft, discard one bean over left shoulder. With needle and thread, string them like beads, interspersing with capers, raspberries, and pearl onions. Garnish with chili powder and lime juice.

Tie the fondue necklace loosely around the throat of a loved one, allowing the center bean to dangle in the angle of Louis. Dine, then relax and enjoy the post prandial 21-bean salute.

REMARKS ON BEANS
COMPILED BY BAXTER BLACK

"Presentation is half the meal, which is good 'cause I can't cook."—Baxter Black

"Speak to me of the humble bean,
Of Milagro, of Jack and the stalk.
Whose bold contribution has earned them a place
In the footnote of history's crock."

Recognized by poets, painters, bards, and the literary glitterati like Shakespeare
who said, "A bean by any other name would still . . ."

If a bean were consumed in the forest and no one heard it,
would it still make a sound?

"One small bean for man, one giant bean burrito for mankind."—Armstrong

Gold, frankincense, and pinto beans.

"I never met a bean I didn't like."—Lyndon Beans Johnson

"A fool and his bean are soon parted."—Anonymous

"Quoth the raven, 'Refried beans.'"—Poe

"Hell hath no fury like a bean turned bad."—Congreve

Governor Kathleen Sebelius admits that her family's favorite comfort food is pot roast and that the first time she came to Kansas and had juicy steaks at her in-law's home was the first time she realized how wonderful beef could taste! With beef production in Kansas outpacing wheat and Kansas ranking first nationally in the number of commercial cattle processed at 7.3 million head in 2005, beef is a mainstay of the Kansas diet.

Filet of Beef Bourguignon
—KANSAS GOVERNOR KATHLEEN SEBELIUS

- 1 three-pound filet of beef, trimmed
- Kosher salt
- Freshly ground black pepper
- 3 or 4 tablespoons good olive oil
- ¼ pound bacon, diced
- 2 garlic cloves, minced
- 1 ½ cups good dry red wine such as burgundy or chianti
- 2 cups beef stock
- 1 tablespoon tomato paste
- 1 sprig fresh thyme
- ½ pound pearl onions, peeled
- 8 to 10 carrots, cut diagonally into 1-inch slices
- 3 tablespoons unsalted butter at room temperature, divided
- 2 tablespoons all-purpose flour
- ½ pound mushrooms, sliced ¼ inch thick

Serves 6–8

With a sharp knife, cut the filet crosswise into 1-inch thick slices. Season both sides with salt and pepper. Heat oil in a large, heavy-bottomed pan on medium-high heat. Sauté the slices of beef in batches, cooking 2 to 3 minutes on each side. Remove from pan and set aside on platter.

In the same pan, cook the bacon on medium-low heat 5 minutes, until browned and crisp. Remove bacon and set it aside. Drain all but 2 tablespoons of fat from the pan. Add the garlic and cook 30 seconds. Add red wine to the pan and cook on high heat 1 minute to deglaze, scraping the bottom of the pan. Add beef stock, tomato paste, thyme, 1 teaspoon salt, and ½ teaspoon pepper.

(recipe continues on next page)

Filet of Beef Bourguignon
(continued)

Bring to a boil and cook uncovered on medium-high heat 10 minutes. Strain the sauce and return it to the pan.

Add the onions and carrots and simmer uncovered 20 to 30 minutes, until the sauce is reduced and the vegetables are tender. With a fork, mash 2 tablespoons butter and the flour into a paste and whisk it gently into the sauce. Simmer 2 minutes to thicken.

Meanwhile, cook the mushrooms separately in 1 tablespoon butter and 1 tablespoon oil about 10 minutes, until browned and tender. Add the beef slices, the mushrooms, and the bacon to the pan with the vegetables and sauce. Cover and heat gently 5 to 10 minutes. Do not overcook. Season to taste and serve immediately.

Dodge City was, in her heyday, Queen of the Cowtowns in Kansas. Today Dodge City relives her glorious past for tourists and keeps the spirit of the Old West alive. You can travel to Boot Hill Cemetery, stroll down the streets of Old Dodge, or watch a gunfight. If you look real close, you might even see TV's Marshall Matt Dillon or Miss Kitty walking down the wood sidewalks, or Doc tending to a patient.

Mom's Recipe for Chicken Fried Steak
—JIM SHERER, MAYOR OF DODGE CITY, KANSAS

- 2 pounds of lean round steak, ½-inch thick, run through tenderizer twice
- 2 to 3 packs of saltine crackers (I prefer Zestee), finely crumbled
- 2 to 3 eggs
- ½ cup milk
- Butter-flavored cooking oil (I prefer Crisco), ½-inch deep in skillet
- Lawry's Seasoning salt, lemon pepper, and coarse ground pepper

Gravy
- 3 to 4 tablespoons of flour
- 4 to 6 cups of milk
- Salt and coarse ground pepper to taste

Serves 6 to 8

When purchasing round steak, have the butcher run it through the tenderizer twice—this is very important.

Cut steak into pieces approximately 2 inches by 3 inches. Put saltine crackers in a ziplock bag and with a rolling pin, roll the crackers into fine crumbs. Place the crumbs in a round cake pan. Break eggs into a bowl, add ½ cup of milk and whisk until thoroughly blended.

Dip each piece of meat into the egg mix coating both sides. Then place the meat into the cracker crumb pan and press it into the crumbs on both sides with your fingers so that the cracker crumbs make a good coating on the meat.

(recipe continues on next page)

Mom's Recipe for Chicken Fried Steak
(continued)

The meat will spread out to approximately 3 inches by 4 inches in size. Prepare all of the meat in this manner, stacking the pieces on a platter.

In a large skillet, heat butter-flavored cooking oil at a ½-inch depth over medium-high heat. Place the pieces arranged loosely in pan. Season with Lawry's Seasoning salt, course ground pepper, and lemon pepper. Cook to medium golden brown on both sides. Don't overcook.

Prepare white gravy in the skillet by removing excess oil but be sure to leave 3 or 4 tablespoons on remaining crumbs. Mix 3 to 4 tablespoons of flour in the remaining drippings until all flour is blended with the oil and reaches a paste consistency. Add 4 to 6 cups of milk and stir mixture over a medium to a medium-high heat until it reaches a medium consistency. You might need to add more milk. Season with salt and coarse ground pepper to taste.

Filet Mignon
with Cabernet Peppercorn Sauce
—A Tallgrass Beef Company Favorite

- 6 filet mignon steaks
- 1 cup white mushrooms, chopped
- ½ cup chopped shallots
- 3 tablespoons black peppercorns
- ¼ cup olive oil
- ½ cup red wine, preferably cabernet
- 2 quarts demi glace
- ½ cup heavy cream
- 1 tablespoon beef base
- Cornstarch, as needed
- Salt and pepper

Season both sides of the filets with salt and pepper. Place the filets on the grill at a 45 degree angle to establish good grill marks. Once the filet reaches an internal temperature of 125 to 130 degrees for medium-rare, remove the steak from the grill and let rest about 5 minutes before serving.

Cabernet-Peppercorn Sauce
In a saucepan over medium heat, sauté mushrooms, shallots, and peppercorns in oil. When shallots are tender, deglaze with red wine and reduce by two-thirds. Whisk together the reduction and demi glace until smooth. Whisk in the cream and beef base. Combine a few teaspoons of cornstarch (or more as needed) with a little cold water to make a slurry. Add slurry to the sauce to thicken; cook for 1 minute and then remove from the heat.

Grilled Ribeye Steaks

—A TALLGRASS BEEF COMPANY FAVORITE

- 1 cup soy sauce
- 1 cup sliced green onions
- ½ cup packed brown sugar
- 4 garlic cloves, minced
- ½ teaspoon ground ginger
- ½ teaspoon pepper
- 5 pounds beef ribeye steaks

In a large resealable plastic bag, combine the soy sauce, onions, brown sugar, garlic, ginger, and pepper. Add the steaks. Seal bag and turn to coat; refrigerate for 8 hours or overnight. Drain and discard marinade. Grill steaks, uncovered, over medium-hot heat for 8 to 10 minutes or until the meat reaches desired doneness (for medium-rare, a meat thermometer should read 145 degrees; medium, 160 degrees; well-done, 170 degrees).

Grilled Lime Marinated Flank Steak
with Chipotle Honey Sauce
—A TALLGRASS BEEF COMPANY FAVORITE

- 2 ½ pounds flank steak
- 1 canned chipotle chili pepper
- 2 garlic cloves, chopped
- 1 tablespoon chopped cilantro
- ¼ cup vegetable oil
- ½ cup freshly squeezed lime juice (about 4 limes)

Sauce
- 3 canned chipotle peppers, pureed
- ¼ cup honey
- 2 teaspoons peanut oil
- 2 tablespoons balsamic vinegar
- 2 tablespoons brown mustard
- 10 tablespoons lime juice
- 2 garlic cloves
- 1 teaspoon ground cumin
- Salt and pepper
- Cilantro (optional)

Serves 8

Place the steak in large dish or baking pan. Mix together the chipotle, garlic, cilantro, vegetable oil, and lime juice in a bowl and pour over the steak. Cover, and marinate in the refrigerator for 4 to 6 hours, turning occasionally.

Combine the chipotles, honey, peanut oil, vinegar, mustard, lime juice, garlic, and cumin in a blender or food processor and puree until smooth. Stir in the cilantro (optional) and season with salt and pepper to taste. Remove the steak from the marinade and season with salt and pepper. Grill over high heat for about 5 minutes on each side for medium rare, 7 minutes per side for medium, or to desired doneness. Remove the steak from the grill and let it rest for about 4 minutes. With a sharp knife, thinly slice the steak across the grain, at a sharp angle.

Serve the steak on top of a slice of French bread and accompany each serving with several tablespoons of the sauce.

Strip Steak
with Rosemary Red Wine Sauce

—A Tallgrass Beef Company Favorite

- 4 boneless strip steaks (3 pounds total, 1-inch thick)
- ½ teaspoon salt
- 1 tablespoon cracked black pepper
- 3 tablespoons olive oil
- ¼ cup chopped onion
- 2 tablespoons chopped fresh rosemary leaves
- 2 cloves garlic, finely chopped
- 1 ½ cups dry red wine
- 1 cup canned condensed beef broth
- ½ teaspoon dark brown sugar

Season both sides of the steaks liberally with salt and pepper. Heat oil in large heavy skillet over high heat. Add steaks. Lower heat to medium; cook, turning once, 4 minutes per side for rare, 6 minutes per side for medium-rare, and 8 minutes per side for well-done. Remove to warm platter; keep warm.

Add onion to skillet; cook until browned, stirring 2 minutes. Add half the rosemary, half the garlic, and cook while stirring for 20 seconds. Add wine. Increase heat to high; boil vigorously 2 minutes. Add broth, sugar, and meat juices that have collected on platter. Boil 10 minutes more or until liquid is reduced by half, about 1 cup. Add remaining rosemary and garlic. Pour over steaks and serve.

"My approach to ingredients developed over a long, slow process," Sarah Stegner says. "When I started out as a chef, I knew that the best, freshest flavors came from ingredients produced by local farmers. But I couldn't find farm contacts easily, so my friends in the business helped introduce me to some of them. What a joy! The farmers turned out to be passionate about what they were doing and very perceptive when it comes to what quality means. I began to establish wonderful working relationships with these producers and the momentum grew from there." Stegner continues to incorporate fresh, seasonal produce from small, regional family farms into her menus at Prairie Grass Cafe.

Tallgrass New York Strip Steak
with Shallot Herb Topping
—SARAH STEGNER AND GEORGE BUMBARIS, PRAIRIE GRASS CAFÉ

- 4 twelve-ounce New York strip steaks, completely trimmed
- Salt
- Fresh ground black pepper
- 2 tablespoons olive oil
- ½ cup minced shallots
- 2 tablespoons olive oil
- ½ teaspoon garlic
- ¼ teaspoon salt
- ¼ teaspoon fresh ground black pepper
- 4 tablespoons unsalted butter, room temperature
- 4 tablespoons rough chopped flat leaf parsley
- ½ cup Panko Flakes bread crumbs
- 1 tablespoon lemon juice
- 4 tablespoons grated parmesan cheese

Preheat oven to 400 degrees. In a small sauté pan over medium heat cook the shallots until tender in olive oil. Add the garlic, salt, and pepper. Cook for another 3 minutes stirring regularly. Remove from the pan and allow to cool.

In a small mixing bowl use a paddle to soften the butter. Add the parsley, bread crumbs, lemon juice, parmesan, and shallot mixture. Mix well. Season the steaks with salt and pepper on all sides. In a large pan over high heat cook the steaks in 2 tablespoons of olive oil. Cook on all sides until the steak is brown and forms a crust. Transfer to a baking pan and finish cooking the meat to desired temperature in a 400 degree oven. Remove from the oven and allow the meat to rest for 5 minutes.

Set your oven on broil. Divide the shallot topping among the steaks. Spread evenly over the top. Return the steaks to the baking pan and put in the oven under the broiler. Cook for a few minutes until the topping becomes golden brown.

Shepherd's Pie Prairie Grass Café Style

—SARAH STEGNER AND GEORGE BUMBARIS, PRAIRIE GRASS CAFÉ

- 2 pounds Tallgrass chuck eye roll cut into 1-inch chunks, fat and sinew removed
- Salt
- Fresh ground black pepper
- 2 tablespoons olive oil
- 1 cup diced onion
- 1 tablespoon chopped garlic
- 1 cup chopped fresh skinned and seeded tomatoes
- 1 cup carrots peeled and large dice
- 1 cup celery large dice
- 1 teaspoon fresh thyme, leaves removed from stem
- 3 cups chicken stock (unseasoned)
- 3 cups demi glace
- 4 bay leaves
- 1 cup blanched swiss chard

Topping
- 4 cups potato purée
- ¼ cup parsnip purée
- ⅛ cup butternut squash purée
- 2 tablespoons whole butter
- 1 cup chicken stock
- Salt
- Fresh ground black pepper

Season the beef with salt and pepper. Sear the meat in olive oil in a large hot pan over medium-high heat. Stir occasionally until the meat is browned on all sides. Remove the meat from the pan and sauté the onions until tender. Add the garlic, carrots, and celery. Return the meat to the pan. Add the chicken stock and demi glace. Cover and cook slowly until the meat is tender. Taste and adjust seasoning. Add the swiss chard and place in four individual oven proof crocks.

Topping
Mix together all ingredients. Divide into 4 portions and spread on top of the braised meat. Place under the broiler for a few minutes or until top is golden brown.

Note that you may have quite a bit of butternut squash purée left over. You can freeze leftover purée in an ice cube tray and save it for other recipes. Or, you may find prepackaged purée at the grocery store.

Harry Caray's Restaurant, named for the late Hall of Fame baseball announcer, opened on October 23, 1987, and has become one of the most nationally recognized restaurants in the Midwest. This legendary Italian steak house serves the finest prime, aged steaks and chops in a truly warm "Chicago" atmosphere. Harry Caray's has won numerous awards including "Best steak house" by the *Chicago Tribune*'s Dining Poll and *Wine Spectator*'s prestigious "Award of Excellence" every year since 1989, and has been ranked continuously in the top 100 highest grossing restaurants in America. The friendly, energetic atmosphere embodies the amiable personality of the restaurant's namesake. The combination of mahogany paneling, white tablecloths, and a veritable museum of baseball history creates a warm and casual elegance.

8-oz Tallgrass Filet
with Lobster Mashed Potatoes and Red Wine Demi Glace
—EXECUTIVE CHEF PAUL KATZ, HARRY CARAY'S RESTAURANT

Steak

- 4 eight-ounce Tallgrass filets
- 2 ounces olive oil
- 3 tablespoons Lawry's Seasoning Salt
- 1 tablespoon ground black pepper
- 16 asparagus stalks

Serves 4

Steak

Brush each steak with olive oil and season with Lawry's Seasoning Salt and black pepper. Heat a sauté pan over high heat. Pan sear on each side until browned to seal in the flavor. Transfer the pan into a 450 degree oven and bake to desired temperature (Approximately 8 minutes for medium-rare, 12 minutes for medium). Before plating, cut off the asparagus tips and blanch in boiling water.

(recipe contiues on next page)

8-oz Tallgrass Filet
(continued)

Red Wine Demi Glace
- 2 cups red wine
- 4 shallots, chopped
- 1 bay leaf
- 3 cups veal stock (recipe follows)
- 1 pinch cracked peppercorns
- Salt and pepper to taste

Lobster Mashed Potatoes
- 6 large Idaho russet potatoes, peeled
- 2 ounces cooked lobster meat
- 6 cups water
- 1 stick of butter
- 1 cup heavy cream

Red Wine Demi Glace
Preheat the oven to 450 degrees. In a saucepot, combine the red wine, shallots, bay leaf, and peppercorns and reduce by three-fourths. Add the veal stock and bring to a boil. Add the salt and pepper to taste.

Lobster Mashed Potatoes
In a medium stockpot, combine the potatoes and enough water to float the potatoes 2 inches off the bottom of the pot. Bring to a low boil for 40 minutes or until you can easily separate the potatoes with a fork. Strain off the liquid and add the butter and salt and pepper to taste. Mash the potatoes, adding the heavy cream until the mixture reaches the desired consistency. Fold the lobster meat into the potatoes.

Serve the filets atop the lobster mashed potatoes and pool the red wine demi glace sauce around the Tallgrass filet. Garnish with cooked asparagus tips.

Homemade Veal Stock

—EXECUTIVE CHEF PAUL KATZ, HARRY CARAY'S RESTAURANT

- 5 pounds veal bones, cut or split into 3-inch pieces
- 8 ounces carrots, rough cut
- 8 ounces celery, rough cut
- 1 pound onion, rough cut
- 8 ounces tomato purée
- 6 parsley stems
- 2 ½ gallons water
- 1 bay leaf
- 6 peppercorns
- ½ ounce fresh herbs (thyme, rosemary, and others)
- Salt and pepper

Makes 6 cups

Preheat the oven to 450 degrees. Place the bones in a roasting pan and sprinkle with the salt and pepper. Place in the oven and brown. Remove the bones from the roasting pan and place in the stock pot. Add the water (bones should be covered in water) and the seasonings. In the roasting pan add the vegetables and place over heat to brown. After browning add 2 cups of the water to deglaze the pan. Pour the vegetables and the juices into the stock pot, scrape out the pan. Using high heat, bring to a boil and add the remaining ingredients. Reduce heat to simmer the stock. Using a ladle, skim the fat off the surface of the stock (repeat several times). The stock should simmer for at least 6 hours until it has flavor and brown color. The stock can be fortified with beef base to obtain a richer flavor. Add the salt and pepper to taste.

You've never stepped into a grill so energetic, so on the edge . . . so on the frontier . . . as Frontera Grill. Frontera swings casual, like an American grill. But it also rollicks with a vibrant, boisterous Mexican rhythm. Its walls radiate sun-baked colors. The paintings and sculptures leap to your eyes and make you laugh. Together they invite you to an ever-young fiesta. And the food? Frontera Grill uses beautiful ingredients, often organic and custom-grown, to bring to you the bold flavors and immediate freshness that jump off the tongue—just as it does in Mexico.

Bistec Encebollado
Slivered Beef with Well-Browned Onions
—RICK BAYLESS, FRONTERA GRILL

"This makes a substantial taco filling and a great casual supper. This recipe is from our first cookbook, Authentic Mexican—now twenty years old!" —Rick Bayless

- 1 pound thin-cut pan-fryable steaks like those called sandwich steaks or flip steak, or even skirt steaks
- Salt and freshly ground black pepper, as desired
- About 3 tablespoons vegetable oil
- 1 large onion, diced or sliced
- 2 large cloves garlic, peeled and minced

Yields about 2 cups, enough for 12 tacos, serving 4 as a light main course

Trim the beef of excess fat and sprinkle with salt and pepper. Over medium-high, heat enough vegetable oil to nicely coat the bottom of a large, heavy skillet. When it is searingly hot, brown the steak for 1 to 2 minutes on each side; for cuts like skirt, be careful not to cook past medium-rare. Remove to a wire rack set over a plate and keep warm in a low oven; reduce the heat under the skillet to medium.

(recipe continues on next page)

Bistec Encebollado (continued)

Add the onion to the skillet and cook, stirring frequently, until a deep golden-brown, about 10 minutes. Stir in the garlic and cook 2 minutes longer.

Cut the meat into thin strips (across the grain, for skirt steak); for tougher cuts of meat, cut into ½-inch pieces. When the onion mixture is ready, add the beef to the skillet and stir until heated through. Season with salt and serve in a deep, warm bowl.

COOK'S NOTES FROM RICK BAYLESS

Searing the Meat: If you sear the meat in a hot pan, you'll get a nice flavor and a good crust; if the pan isn't hot, you'll find pale meat simmering in its juices.

The Meat: The Mexican *bisteces* often used in this preparation are taken from the tougher cuts (frequently the round) and pounded. Choose thin round steaks (often sold as breakfast steaks, sandwich steaks, flip steaks, wafer steaks, or perhaps under other names) and pound them if necessary; or choose any thin steak tender enough to pan-fry. I like trimmed skirt steak because of its flavor and texture. Frequently, Mexican street vendors use the sheets of thin sliced beef (*cecina*); it's tougher, so they chop it into small pieces.

Minor variations on the theme: The meat may be marinated. It may also be fried in olive oil. Red onions may replace white, 4 roasted cloves of garlic could be used instead of raw ones. And strips of just about any roasted and peeled chili pepper could be stirred in with the meat.

Chef Michel Nischan teams up with Hollywood legend Paul Newman to offer a restaurant that will focus on a true rebirth of American Heritage foods and recipes, The Dressing Room. From "Yankee Pot Roast" to "Hook and Line Chatham Cod" to "Cox Orange Pippin Apple" desserts, the restaurant will reinvigorate recipes that once defined American food culture. Located in historic Westport, Connecticut, next to the famed Westport County Playhouse, this restaurant preserves the true flavors of American cuisine in every tempting bite. You can make this Beef Short Rib Pot Roast with Tallgrass Beef for a flavorful, healthy family meal.

Beef Short Rib Pot Roast
—Chef Michel Nischan, The Dressing Room

- 2 boneless beef short ribs
- 1 ½ quarts fortified veal stock
- 6 ounces peeled salsify, cut into 3-inch pieces
- 4 ounces peeled medium carrots, cut into 3-inch pieces
- 4 ounces partially peeled celery ribs, cut into 3-inch pieces
- 10 ounces peeled cipollini onions
- 8 small to medium Yukon potatoes, peeled
- ¼ cup fresh sour cream
- ¼ cup freshly grated horseradish root
- 1 tablespoon freshly squeezed lemon juice
- 2 tablespoons freshly shaved chives
- 2 cups fried salsify shavings
- Sea salt and freshly ground pepper to season

Generously season the ribs on all sides with salt and pepper. Let stand to weep for 15 minutes. In the meantime, heat a dry roasting pan just large enough to hold the ribs with some room left over. Add the ribs to the hot pan and sear well on all sides until the ribs are deeply browned. Remove the ribs and sear all of the vegetables in individual groups (all the salsify together, all the carrots together and so on) until sweated and lightly browned.

Set the vegetables aside and return the ribs to the pan and cover with the fortified veal stock. Bring to a simmer. Skim well then cover and transfer to a preheated 200 degree oven.

(recipe continues on next page)

Beef Short Rib Pot Roast
(continued)

Cook 4 hours at 200 degrees or until the meat just begins to become tender. Gently remove the meat from the braising liquid and keep warm.

Blanch each set of vegetables until they are just softened in the braising liquid. Some will take longer than others so I recommend blanching them individually. As each set of vegetables finish cooking, set them aside on a holding tray.

Return the ribs to the braising liquid, which has now been fortified with the flavor of the vegetables. Increase the oven heat to 300 degrees and cook, covered, 1 to 1½ hours, or until the ribs are tender. Remove the pan from the oven and allow to cool to room temperature. Gently remove the ribs from the braising liquid, cover and refrigerate about an hour or until the collagen in the ribs sets firm. Trim and cut the ribs into nicely shaped portions.

In the meantime, strain the braising liquid through a fine chinois into a medium saucepot. Reduce the sauce by about half. Season to taste with salt and pepper. Arrange the individual rib portions in large oven-proof serving casserole, or into individual serving crocks. Surround with equal amounts of the blanched vegetables. Pour the reduced braising liquid over and return to the oven to heat through.

While heating, blend the sour cream, horseradish, and lemon juice together. Season to taste with salt and pepper. Remove the roasts from the oven and top each roast with some of the sour cream. Sprinkle over with shaved chives and garnish with the salsify shavings.

Braised Tallgrass Beef Short Ribs
Asian-Style with Baby Bok Choy, Shiitake Mushrooms, and Jasmine Rice

—CHEF DAVID BURNS, THE STADIUM CLUB AT WRIGLEY FIELD

Short ribs

- 32-ounce boneless Tallgrass beef short ribs, trimmed, cut into 4 eight-ounce portions
- 3 tablespoons of vegetable oil
- 1 medium onion, peeled, cut into ½ inch pieces
- 2 medium carrots, peeled, trimmed, cut into ½ inch pieces
- 3 stalks of celery, peeled, trimmed, and cut into ½ inch pieces
- 8 ounces shiitake mushrooms, stems removed, rough chopped
- 2 ounces ginger, peeled and rough chopped
- 4 cloves of garlic, peeled and chopped
- 2 sprigs of thyme
- 2 tablespoons of tomato paste
- 2 bay leaves
- 8 ounces cabernet sauvignon

Serves 4

Center a rack in the oven and preheat oven to 325 degrees. Heat the oil in a Dutch oven or large casserole (large enough to fit all the beef evenly in the pot) over a medium to high heat. Season the Tallgrass short ribs with salt and pepper.

Dredge the ribs in the flour and sear in the pot for about 4–5 minutes on each side, until well browned. Remove Tallgrass short ribs from the pan. Remove all but 1 tablespoon of fat from the pot, lower the heat to medium and toss in the onions, carrots, celery, thyme, and bay leaf. Sauté for about 5 minutes. Add shiitake mushrooms, cook for 2 minutes. Add the garlic, ginger, and five spice; continue cooking for 5 minutes. Add the tomato paste and cook for 1 minute until well blended. Add the red wine and reduce to 1 cup. Add the teriyaki and soy sauce. Put the short ribs back into the pot; add the stock. Cover pot with a lid and bring to a soft boil.

(ingredients and recipe continue on next page)

Braised Tallgrass Beef Short Ribs
(continued)

- 2 ounces teriyaki sauce
- 2 ounces low sodium soy sauce
- ½ ounce Asian Five Spice
- 2 quarts beef or chicken stock, or low sodium beef or chicken broth
- Kosher Salt
- Black pepper
- 4 ounces flour for dredging

Garnish
- 8 ounces shiitake mushrooms, stems removed and cut into thin strips
- 4 baby bok choy (1 per serving), cut into quarters and rinsed
- 1 ounce finely chopped ginger
- 1 ounce finely chopped garlic
- 2 ounces chopped green onions
- 1 tablespoon of vegetable oil

Jasmine Rice
- 2 cups Jasmine rice
- 3 cups water
- Salt and pepper

Place pot in oven and let cook for about 1 hour until tender enough to be easily pierced with a fork. Carefully remove the Tallgrass short ribs from the pot, place on a serving platter and keep warm. Place the pot on a burner and reduce sauce until it is nappé (able to coat the back of a spoon evenly). Strain the sauce through a strainer on top of the short ribs, discard the solids.

Garnish
Heat the oil in a medium sauté pan on a medium heat. When oil is hot, add the mushrooms and cook for 2 minutes; add the bok choy and cook for another 4 minutes. Add the ginger, garlic, and green onions, and cook for 1 minute.

Jasmine Rice
Heat small pot on medium heat, add oil, sauté rice for 2 minutes. Add water and salt and pepper to taste. Cover and place in a 350 degree oven for 15 to 18 minutes or cook on top of the stove on low heat for 15 minutes.

On a serving plate, place jasmine rice in the center. Place short ribs on top of the rice, top off with garnish. Pour braising liquid over short ribs. Enjoy.

Black Pepper–Crusted Standing Rib Roast au Jus

—Chef Colin Crowley, Terlato Wines

Boning the roast makes slicing the meat much easier at serving time. Have your butcher remove the backbone, or chine, from the whole rack and cut the meat off the ribs in one piece, and then tie the meat back onto the bones. The roast can be served on or off the bones.

- 1 eight-and-a-half pound Tallgrass Beef standing rib roast (weight with bones), top fat trimmed
- Vegetable oil
- 12 tablespoons (1 ½ sticks) unsalted butter, room temperature
- 2 tablespoons cracked or coarsely ground black pepper (To crack whole peppercorns, enclose them in a resealable plastic bag and crush slightly with a meat mallet.)
- 4 large garlic cloves, minced
- ½ teaspoon salt
- 2 ¼ cups beef broth
- ½ cup dry red wine

Serves 12

Place roast, fat side up, in roasting pan. Brush exposed ends of roast with vegetable oil. Sprinkle roast lightly all over with salt. Mix 8 tablespoons butter, 2 tablespoons cracked pepper, minced garlic, and ½ teaspoon salt in small bowl. Reserve 2 tablespoons pepper butter for sauce. Spread remaining pepper butter all over top (fat side) of roast. (Can be prepared 1 day ahead. Cover roast and reserved pepper butter separately; chill.)

Position rack in bottom third of oven and preheat to 350 degrees. Roast rib roast until instant-read thermometer inserted into thickest part of meat registers 125 degrees for medium-rare, about 2 hours 45 minutes. Transfer roast to platter and cover loosely with foil; let rest 30 minutes (temperature will rise slightly as roast stands).

(recipe continues on next page)

Black Pepper-Crusted Standing Rib Roast au Jus
(continued)

Strain pan juices from roasting pan into measuring cup. Skim off any fat from top of pan juices; discard fat. Return pan juices to roasting pan; set pan over 2 burners. Add broth and wine to roasting pan and boil over high heat until liquid is reduced to 1¼ cups, scraping up any browned bits from bottom of pan, about 6 minutes. Whisk in reserved pepper butter and remaining 4 tablespoons plain butter.

Slice roast and serve with sauce. Garnish serving platter with roasted red onions and one large bunch watercress.

Whole Roasted Beef Sirloin
with Chasseur Sauce

—CHEF COLIN CROWLEY, TERLATO WINES

- 1 four-pound Tallgrass Beef prime sirloin strip roast, cleaned of fat and cut in half lengthwise
- 4 tablespoons butter
- 3 cups crimini mushrooms, diced
- 6 shallots, minced
- 12 ounces red wine
- 6 tablespoons brandy
- 4 cups veal demi glace (may substitute with 3 cups demi glace and 1 cup beef or chicken stock)
- 2 cups tomatoes, diced
- 1 tablespoon parsley, chopped
- Salt and pepper

Serves 6

Sirloin

Coat meat with olive oil and season with salt and pepper. In a preheated 350-degree oven roast for approximately 30 minutes, or until internal temperature reaches 130 degrees for medium rare.

Chasseur Sauce

Melt butter in a heavy sauce pan. Add shallots and mushrooms, sauté till butter is absorbed. Add wine and bring to a boil, then simmer until reduced to almost dry 10 to 15 minutes. Add brandy and flame. Add veal demi glace and bring to a light simmer. Add parsley and tomatoes to finish. Season with salt and pepper.

REMARKS ON DEMI GLACE

One of the traditional French sauces, demi glace is considered quite complicated to prepare at home. However, there are several pre-made varieties available through gourmet catalogs (Chef Colin Crowley recommends the Allen Brothers catalog and Provimi Veal's demi glace.) Be forewarned, pre-made demi glace is expensive, so you may want to wait for a special occasion.

Beef Bourguignon

—Chef Colin Crowley, Terlato Wines

- 3 ½ pounds Tallgrass beef steak or tenderloin tips, cut into 2-inch pieces
- 1 large carrot, 1 large onion, peeled and cut into chunks
- 2 sticks celery, roughly chopped
- 2 bottles pinot noir
- 2 sprigs fresh thyme
- 1 head garlic, cut in half horizontally
- 4 bay leaves

Entrée
- 2 ounces unsalted butter
- ½ pound of applewood smoked bacon, cut in half
- 3 tablespoons plain flour
- 1 large carrot, 1 large onion, 2 sticks celery, peeled and diced
- ½ pint beef stock

Garnish
- ½ pound of applewood smoked bacon, diced and rendered
- 12 ounces crimini mushrooms, sauteed
- Fresh chopped flatleaf parsley

Serves 6

Marinade
Combine first 8 ingredients in a bowl and refrigerate overnight.

Entrée
Remove meat from marinade, pat dry and reserve the liquid. Season the meat with salt and pepper and dredge with the flour. Meanwhile, in a hot sauté pan heat the butter until melted. Sear the meat on all sides until brown, add bacon. Deglaze with 1 cup of the marinade. Pour beef stock over, add diced vegetables and adjust seasoning. Cook in a 275-degree oven for approximately 2½ to 3 hours, or until the meat is tender. Garnish with bacon, mushrooms and parsley.

Can be served with egg noodles, rice, or potatoes.

Braised Short Ribs
with Morel Mushroom and Cannellini Bean Ragout
—Chef Colin Crowley, Terlato Wines

- 6 Tallgrass Beef short ribs, approximately one pound each
- 1 large carrot, unpeeled and roughly chopped
- 1 medium onion, unpeeled and roughly chopped
- 3 ribs of celery, roughly chopped
- ½ head of garlic, halved horizontally
- ¼ cup dried porcini mushrooms, reconstituted
- 1 teaspoon fennel seed
- 1 tablespoon black peppercorns
- 1 teaspoon dried thyme
- 1 cup red wine
- 1 quart veal stock, preferably unseasoned
- Olive oil
- Salt and pepper

Serves 6 to 8

In a large, uncovered stockpot, soak the dried beans in water (to cover by 2 inches) overnight. Alternatively, bring beans and water to a boil, turn off heat and let sit for 1 hour.

Season short ribs with salt and pepper. Cover bottom of a 4-quart braising pan with ⅛ inch of olive oil and heat until hot, but not smoking. Brown ribs a few minutes on each side until browned and set aside.

Drain the fat from the pan, leaving a tablespoon or two. Add the roughly chopped carrot, onion, celery, and garlic and sauté over high heat until vegetables start to brown. Add porcinis, fennel seed, peppercorns, and thyme and cook until vegetables are well caramelized. Add wine and reduce until almost dry. Add stock, check and readjust seasoning and cook until stock is heated through.

(ingredients and recipe continue on next page)

Braised Short Ribs
(continued)

Ragout
- 3 cups dried cannellini beans
- 2 quarts chicken stock
- ½ large carrot, peeled and diced small
- ½ medium onion, peeled and diced small
- 1 rib celery, diced small
- 1 cup fresh morel mushrooms
- 1 shallot, minced
- 1 tablespoon butter
- ½ cup grape tomatoes, halved
- Salt and pepper

Add short ribs (stock should be about three-fourths of the way up the sides of the ribs) and cook in 300-degree oven for about 3 hours.

When short ribs are halfway done, drain the beans and rinse once with clean water. Return beans to pot and add chicken stock and diced carrot, onion, and celery. Bring to simmer and cook over low heat until beans are tender (1 to 1½ hours). Remove from heat and set aside. In a medium sauté pan, sauté the shallot in the butter until translucent, add the morels, season with salt and pepper, and cook until almost dry.

Remove short ribs from oven and add 1 cup of the braising liquid along with the tomatoes to the morels. Simmer until tomatoes begin to soften, stir into beans and heat through. Remaining braising liquid and vegetables can be discarded. Halve each short rib and serve each person 1–2 halves over a generous scoop of the ragout. Bones can be removed for a more refined presentation. Simple sautéed escarole makes a wonderful additional accompaniment.

Grilled Beef Tenderloin Cobb Salad

—CHARLIE TROTTER, CHARLIE TROTTER'S

This has to be one of my all-time favorite salads, because of the unrestrained variety of flavors and textures. Traditionally a cobb salad is made with chicken, but I use grilled beef because I prefer a little more substance. I lay out the ingredients in the traditional manner, in rows on a bed of lettuce. You can, of course, toss everything together and not bother with this special presentation. The flavors and textures would certainly be the same, but sometimes the striking composition of a finished dish is reward enough for the extra trouble.

- 1 shallot, minced
- ⅓ cup freshly squeezed lemon juice
- 2 tablespoons chopped fresh chives
- 1 cup olive oil
- Salt and pepper
- 1 ⅓ cups peeled and diced red and yellow tomatoes
- 8 cups mesclun mix
- 8 slices prosciutto, julienned
- 16 quail eggs, soft-boiled, peeled, and quartered
- 8 ounces beef tenderloin, grilled, cooled, and diced
- 1 ⅓ cups diced avocado
- 1 ⅓ cups crumbled blue cheese
- 12 grilled scallions, chilled and chopped
- 4 tablespoons 1-inch pieces chives

Serves 4

Vinaigrette

Place the shallot and lemon juice in a small bowl. Slowly whisk in the olive oil, fold in the chopped chives, and season to taste with salt and pepper.

Tomatoes

Toss the diced tomatoes with 2 tablespoons of the vinaigrette and season to taste with salt and pepper.

Greens

Toss the mesclun mix with half of the vinaigrette and season to taste with salt and pepper.

(recipe continues on next page)

Grilled Beef Tenderloin Cobb Salad
(continued)

Assembly

Arrange some of the mesclun greens to create a bed in the center of each plate. Arrange some of the prosciutto in a vertical line along the far left side of the greens. Next to the prosciutto, arrange some of the quail eggs, avocado, tomatoes, beef tenderloin, blue cheese, and scallions each in individual vertical lines to completely cover the mesclun mix. Top with freshly ground black pepper and sprinkle with the chive pieces. Drizzle the remaining vinaigrette over the salad.

A Day in the Saddle on the Red Buffalo Ranch

Red angus on the Red Buffalo Ranch. The day begins with cattle searching for tender grasses, soaking in the sun's rays.

A siren-equipped feed truck calls the cattle and the earth shakes with the pounding of their mighty hooves.

Attracted by the sound and the hopes of extra hay, the cattle line up and make a run for the truck.

Cattle drives today on the Red Buffalo Ranch in Sedan, Kansas can be as simple as running the cattle from the barn out to the pasture, then back home at the end of the day. That's quite different from the nineteenth-century experience. In 1885, at the age of seventeen, Frederick Albert Scott left the Fort Worth area seeking employment on a cattle ranch. Driven by a desire to work hard, climb the ladder of success, and please his employers, Scott traveled to the untamed Texas Panhandle. Riding a 600-pound bay horse three hundred miles in seven days to reach Charles Goodnight's range, he carried a slicker for bedding and a paltry amount of rations. With a starting monthly salary of $25, he worked for one year as a herd cowboy. Within that year he proved to be a hard worker and was given

Ron Ladner, a Tallgrass Beef Company cowboy and ultrasound technician, works the herd.

The herd moves down the gravel road.

Once in line and on the move the cattle work their way toward the gate and for the open road.

a hefty raise. Now earning $30 per month he truly felt that he was a king on horseback. After five months, Scott was put at the head of the point of a herd and was bound for Dodge City, queen of the Kansas cow towns.

Scott remembered that "eleven hundred steers were taken on this thirty-day trip; a few old cows were taken." With eight men on the trail and a chuck wagon loaded with supplies and 50 gallons of water, the trail drive began. Each man would sleep under a tarp, sometimes waking in the morning to dust off several inches of snow or dirt that had blown in during the night. Each day the herd made 12 to 15 miles, and at night were calmed down until the next day's drive began. The slightest noise

Swinging the lariat, Ron Ladner moves the cattle down the road toward their destination.

Do we have any mail? Cattle are curious about the world around them.

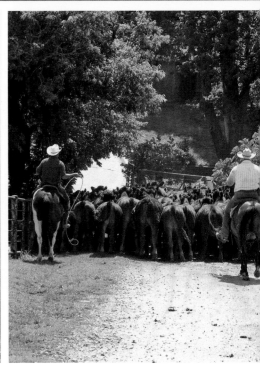

Through the gate safe and sound, a day's work well done.

or movement could set a herd to stampede—the stumbling of a horse, the striking of a match, the smoking of a cigarette. Men were more afraid of the stampede than anything else on the drive. By the time the drive to Dodge City was complete, cattle were loaded twenty-eight head to a car and shipped to points east for slaughter and processing.

The cowboys received their pay at the end of the drive. With pockets brimming with money, they either gambled, drank or ate it away in Dodge, then returned home to start the process again. Given that the JA Ranch branded 45,000 calves in 1885 alone, one can surmise that these cowboys lived their lives on the trail, open and free.

Experience the West

Now that you have seen and experienced the grandeur of the American West, take the great newspaper editor Horace Greeley's advice and "go west!" The locations and organizations listed here contributed their time, expertise, or materials to help make this book come to life! Small towns and county museums are treasure troves of information waiting for you.

California
Autry National Center
Institute for the Study of the American West
Autry and Braun Research Libraries
4700 Western Heritage Way
Los Angeles, CA 90027-1462
www.autrynationalcenter.org/

Kansas
Baxter Springs Heritage Center and Museum
740 East Avenue P.O. Box 514
Baxter Springs, KS 66713
620-856-2385
http://home.4state.com/~heritagectr/

Caldwell, KS
www.caldwellkansas.com/city_home1.htm

Center for Great Plains Studies
www.emporia.edu/cgps/

Chase County Historical Society Museum
301 Broadway
Cottonwood Falls, KS 66845
620-273-8500

Dodge City, KS
www.visitdodgecity.org/

Drover's Mercantile
119 N. Douglas
Ellsworth, KS 67439
877-376-8377
www.droversmercantile.com

Experience the Kansas Flint Hills
www.kansasflinthills.travel/

The Flying W Ranch
Josh Hoy
RR1
Cedar Point, KS 66843
620-340-3208
www.flying-w-ranch.net

Fort Scott National Historic Site
1 Old Fort Blvd.
Fort Scott, KS 66701
620-223-0310
www.nps.gov/fosc/

Kansas Cattle Town Coalition
www.kansascattletowns.org/

Kansas State Historical Society and
History Museum
6425 SW Sixth Avenue
Topeka, KS 66615-1099
785-272-8681
www.kshs.org

Little House on the Prairie
The Official Historical Site
Near Independence, KS
www.littlehouseontheprairie.com
620-289-4238

Old Cowtown Museum
1865 Museum Blvd.
Wichita, KS 67203
316-660-1871
www.oldcowtown.org/

Red Buffalo Ranch
107 E. Main Street
Sedan, KS 67361
620-725-4022
www.theredbuffalo.com/

Tallgrass Beef Company
103 East Main Street, Suite 1
Sedan, KS 67361
877-822-8283

Tallgrass Prairie National Preserve
P.O. Box 585
Cottonwood Falls, KS 66845
620-273-8494
www.nps.gov/tapr/

The Three Barns
1780 Junction Road
Sedan, KS 67361

Missouri
The Roy Rogers and Dale Evans Museum
3950 Green Mountain Drive
Branson, MO 65616
www.royrogers.com/

Oklahoma
Chisholm Trail Heritage Center
1000 Chisholm Trail Parkway
Duncan, OK 73534
580-252-6692
www.onthechisholmtrail.com/index.htm

National Cowboy and Western Heritage
Museum
1700 NE 63rd Street
Oklahoma City, OK 73111
www.nationalcowboymuseum.org/

Oklahoma Historical Society
2401 N. Laird Avenue
Oklahoma City, OK 73105
405-522-5248
www.okhistory.org/

Prairie Song
Kenneth and Marilyn Moore Tate
402621 West 1600 Road
Dewey, OK 74029
918-534-3435
www.prairiesong.net

The Rushing Wagon
Trammel and Susan Rushing
10650 N. Banner Road
El Reno, OK 73036
405-262-6721

Will Rogers Memorial Museum
1720 West Will Rogers Blvd.
Claremore, OK 74018
918-341-0719
www.willrogers.org/

Woolaroc Ranch, Museum and
Wildlife Preserve
1925 Woolaroc Ranch Road
Bartlesville, OK 74003
918-336-0307, 1-888-966-5276
www.woolaroc.org

Texas
Palo Duro Canyon State Park
www.palodurocanyon.com

Panhandle Plains Museum
www.panhandleplains.org/

Chapter Notes

Chapter 1

The Journals of the Lewis and Clark Expedition. 2005. University of Nebraska Press/ University of Nebraska–Lincoln Libraries– Electronic Text Center. 5 Oct. 2005. http://lewisandclarkjournals.unl.edu.

John Bradbury, *Travels in the Interior of America, in the Years 1809, 1810, and 1811, 2nd ed.* (London: Sherwood, Neely, and Jones, 1819), 50.

William E. Foley and Charles David Rice, "Visiting the President: An Exercise in Jeffersonian Indian Diplomacy," *The American West*, Vol. 16, No. 6 (November–December 1979), 6.

Adolph Roenigk, with John C. Baird, *Pioneer History of Kansas* (Lincoln: Kansas, 1933), 168.

Recipes for We-Gi, Wild Grape Dumplings, Ah Hah Jumba Tuklaygee, Pxashikana, Seminole Parched Corn, Poke, and Indian Baked Raccoon provided by the Baxter Springs Heritage Center, Baxter Springs, Kansas.

Scrapple, Fried Meat Pies, Chi-bonne' Hamburger recipes were provided by Connie L. Pruitt, Marland Estate, Ponca City, Oklahoma.

Pemmican recipe taken from Randolph P. Marcy, Capt. U.S. Army, *The Prairie Traveler: Handbook for Overland Expeditions with Maps, Illustrations, and Itineraries of the Principal Routes Between the Mississippi and the Pacific* (Published by the authority of the War Department, 1859), Chapter 1.

Chapter 2

Captain Charles W. Porter, Journal of Captain Charles W. Porter Co. F 3rd Wisconsin Cavalry, taken from typescript copy at Fort Scott National Historic Site, Fort Scott, Kansas. Original journal located at Wisconsin State Historical Society, Charles W. Porter Collection.

Joseph Walker, post surgeon. Report of post surgeon taken from a typescript copy at Fort Scott National Historic Site, Fort Scott, Kansas. Original documents located at the National Archives and Records Administration.

Letter Lt. Ewell to Wife Becca, Fort Scott, October 3rd, 1845, typescript copy at Fort Scott National Historic Site. Original located at the Library of Congress, Lt. Ewell collection.

Recipes for Texacus and Fricassee of Beef from the collections of the Fort Scott National Historic Site.

The Cooks Creed, Kitchen Philosophy, Army Bread Recipe, Irish Stew, Buffalo Tongue, Dried Bean Soup, Remarks on Meat, Pounded Beef, Bombshells, Cooked Salt Beef, Boiled Salt Beef, Baked Salt Beef, Stewed Salt Beef from The United States Subsistence Department, *Manual for Army Cooks* (Washington, G.P.O., 1883, 1896).

Chapter 3

All quotations from Florence Healy, Viola Catherine Alexander, Emma Kreuter from the Lilla Day Monroe Collection, Kansas State Historical Society, copyright 1982, Joanna L. Stratton, All Rights Reserved, used by permission of Joanna L. Stratton. These women were also featured in Joanna Stratton, *Pioneer Women: Voices from the Kansas Frontier* (New York: Simon and Schuster, 1981).

Josiah L. Gregg, *Commerce of the Prairies: Or the Journal of a Santa Fe Trader, During Eight Expeditions Across The Great Western Prairies, and a residence of nearly nine years in Northern Mexico,* Illustrated with Maps and Engravings, in two volumes (New York: Henry G. Langley, 8 Astor House; London: Wiley and Putnam, 6 Waterloo Place, 1844) Chapter 4, Volume II, 84.

Recipes for Meat Loaf, Meat Rocks, Flank Steak, and Mrs. Peaks's Pineapple Cucumber Salad were taken from the day book of Kitty Hayes Houghton of Cottonwood Falls, Kansas. Used by permission of the Chase County Historical Society, Cottonwood Falls, Kansas.

Remarks on Meat, Roast Beef No. 1, and Spiced Beef taken from *Kansas Home Cook Book*, compiled by Mrs. C.H. Cushing and Mrs. B. Gray (1886) from the personal collection of Carol Sloan, Ponca City, Oklahoma. This cookbook belonged to Ms. Sloan's grandmother. (The copy of the book used for this publication did not have its original citation page.)

Recipes for Roast Beef No. 2, Beef Steaks, Fried Beef Steak, Smothered Steak, French Stew No. 2, Beef á-la-Mode, Fried Rabbit, Baked Prairie Chicken, and Snipe from Hannah Mary Bouvier Peterson, *The national cook book*, By a lady of Philadelphia, A practical housewife; and author of the "Family save-all" (Philadelphia: T. B. Peterson and brothers, 1866).

Recipes for Helen's Baked Hash, Lucine's Five Hour Stew, Lynch's Famous Chili taken from Wilma Kurtis and Anita Gold, *Prairie Recipes and Kitchen Antiques: Original Recipes Gathered from the Pioneer Families at Wayside, Kansas the site of the Original Little House on the Prairie* (Bonus Books, 1992). Used by permission of the Kurtis family.

Recipes for Apple Dumplings, Liver and Onions, and Good Brown Stew and reminiscences provided by Judy Tolbert, Sedan, Kansas.

Recipes for Barbecue Style Meatloaf, Chili Stew, Beef Jerky, and Fresh Mountain Oysters from Mattie Wright, Nancy Dye and Betsy Dye, *Recipes Remedies Recollections* (Breckenridge American, 1976). Published by permission of the Breckenridge American.

Letter Ellen D. Goodnow to Harriet Goodnow, May 18, 1856, Territorial Kansas Online collection (www.territorialkansasonline.org)

Chapter 4

Myra Hull, "Cowboy Ballads," *Kansas State Historical Society Quarterly*, February 1939 (Vol. 8, No. 1) 35–60.

All quotations from Mattie Huffman Emily Biggs in this chapter are from the Lilla Day Monroe Collection, Kansas State Historical Society, copyright 1982, Joanna L. Stratton, All Rights Reserved, used by permission of Joanna L. Stratton.

Recipes for Ranch House Pot Roast, Frying Pan Supper, Pan Fried Steaks, Helava Chili, Chuckwagon Scrapple, Rice and Onions, and Squirrel Can Stew reprinted with permission of publisher from Scott Gregory, *Sowbelly and Sourdough: Original Recipes from the Trail Drives and Cow Camps of the 1880s* (Caldwell, ID: Caxton Press, 1999).

Hamburger, Hamburg Steak, Pot Roast Old Style taken from *Ladies of the First Baptist Church of Amarillo, Amarillo Cook Book*, ca. 1909.

All quotations from Reno to the *Titusville Herald* from Paul H. Giddens, "News from Kansas in 1870," *Kansas State Historical Society Quarterly*, May 1938 (Vol. 7., No. 2) 170–182.

All quotations from Jack Bailey from Jack Bailey, *A Texas Cowboy's Journal: Up the Trail to Kansas in 1868* ed. David Dary (Norman: University of Oklahoma Press, 2006), used by permission of the University of Oklahoma Press.

Joseph McCoy, *Sketches of the Cattle Trade of the South West* (Kansas City, MO: Ramsey, Millett and Hudson, 1874).

Recipes for Bacon and Beans, Chili Beef, Sourdough starter, Sourdough Biscuits, Berry cobbler, Pounded steak, and Son of a gun stew provided by Jim Hoy of Emporia, Kansas and his son Josh Hoy of Cedar Point, Kansas.

Recipes for Confederate Coffee Cake, Beef Tips, Smothered Steak, Beef Tenders, Texas Beef Tips, Roast Beef, Cowpoke Beans, Sage Biscuits and Ketcham Canyon Stew courtesy of Trammel Rushing of The Rushing Wagon, El Reno, Oklahoma, private unpublished collection.

Cowboy Beans recipe provided by the Kansas Cattle Town Coalition.

Chapter 5

Recipes for Beef Roll-Ups, Whiskey Butter Sauce, and Broccoli-Cauliflower Salad provided by Judy Tolbert, Sedan, Kansas.

Cowboy Steaks in a Skillet recipe provided by Steve Katz.

Will Rogers Favorite Chili recipe provided by the Will Rogers Memorial Museum, Claremore, Oklahoma.

Homemade Meatloaf recipe and still photo from *Goldmine In The Sky* (1938), courtesy of Autry Qualified Interest Trust and the Autry Foundation.

Pheasant à la King recipe provided by the Frank Phillips Foundation and the Woolaroc Museum, Bartlesville, Oklahoma.

Filet of Beef Bourguignon recipe reprinted from Janet Majure, *Not By Bread Alone: A Sampling of Kansas Food, Art and Culture*, A tribute on the occasion of the 2007 inauguration of the Honorable Kathleen Sebelius as Governor of Kansas, ed. Scott Allegrucci, (Sun Graphics, LLC, 2007), by permission of Governor Kathleen Sebelius.

Mom's Recipe for Chicken Fried Steak, provided by Mayor Jim Sherer, Dodge City, Kansas.

Prairie Grass Café recipes courtesy of Sarah Stegner and George Bumbaris.

Harry Caray's recipes courtesy of Paul Katz.

Frontera Grill recipes courtesy of Rick Bayless.

Wrigley Field Stadium Club recipe courtesy of David Burns.

The Dressing Room recipe courtesy of Michel Nischan.

Terlato Wines recipes courtesy of Chef Colin Crowley.

Charlie Trotter's recipe reprinted from *The Kitchen Sessions with Charlie Trotter*, published by Ten Speed Press, by permission of Charlie Trotter.

Photo Credits

Every effort has been made to correctly attribute all the materials reproduced in this book. If any errors have been made, we will be happy to correct them in future editions.

All photos Michelle M. Martin, except the following on the pages as noted: Baxter Black, 117; Baxter Springs Heritage Center, 8 (bottom); *Goldmine in the Sky* (1938), courtesy of Autry Qualified Interest Trust and the Autry Foundation, 113; Harry Caray's Restaurant, 129; Kansas Heritage Center, 99; Kansas State Historical Society, 28, 48 (bottom); Mark Houser, 127; Marland Grand Home and Estate 101 Ranch Collection, 75 (top); National Cowboy and Western Heritage Museum, 48 (top), 70, 73 (top), 75 (bottom), 76; Office of the Governor, State of Kansas, 120; Renee Comet, 111; Research Division of the Oklahoma Historical Society, 22, 72, 80, 85 (bottom); Tallgrass Beef Company, 17 (top), 35 (middle), 50 (top), 82 (top left), 85 (top), 102, 124, 125; Will Rogers Heritage, Inc, 112; Woolaroc Museum Collection, 12 (right), 73 (bottom), 74, 90 (bottom), 115

Photo Descriptions

8 (bottom), Cowboys and a lone Indian pose for photos near Baxter Springs, KS
12 (right), A portrait of Big Chief, an Osage Chief
22, Clarence W. Turner's ranch feedlot
28, A bull train fording the Smoky Hill River in Kansas, from the Gardner Collection
48 (bottom), Family with a tame elk in Kansas, from the Gardner Collection
70, Studio portrait of an unidentified cowboy, John C. Miller, Denver, CO, ca. 1882, gift of John H. Tillmann
72, Herds and round up in western Oklahoma
73, Ellsworth, Kansas 1867, John Santangelo Collection
74, The annual Cow Thieves and Outlaws event held at Woolaroc brought together those that had lived and loved the life of the cowboy

75 (top), Cattle being driven across the river on the 101 Ranch near Ponca City, OK
75 (bottom), Cowboys Ready to Start, Adolph Seglie, St. Louis, Missouri, 1907, from the Donald C. and Elizabeth M. Dickinson Research Center
76, Unidentified pair of cowboys in studio, photographer unknown, ca. 1882, gift of John H. Tillmann
80, Meal Time at the chuckwagon
85 (bottom), Cowboys eating dinner at Sugg Ranch big pasture, from the Ranch and Range Collection
90 (bottom), Thanksgiving Dinner for the Ranch, from the collection of Frederick Remington.
99, Front Street in Dodge City, Kansas, ca. 1878